# DISPATCHES AGAINST DISPLACEMENT
Field Notes from San Francisco's Housing Wars

D0063096

**Praise for *Dispatches Against Displacement*:**

"James Tracy knows that our dysfunctional housing machine is working as it should: working for the rich. This important history throws sand into the gears of that machine. It is a vision of a better housing system. And it is a defiant story, told from the frontlines of citizens fighting for the right to their city, with lessons that matter for any community aspiring to control its own destiny." —**Raj Patel**, author of *Stuffed and Starved*

"With the insight of a poet and the long-term vision of a seasoned organizer, *Dispatches Against Displacement* weaves together a powerful, instructive, hilarious, and poignant description of how the working class fights back in the City by the Bay." —**Alicia Garza**, National Domestic Workers Alliance

**Praise for James Tracy:**

"James Tracy is a poet and speaker who leaves the audience stunned, then energized." —**Roxanne Dunbar Ortiz**, author of *Outlaw Woman: Memoir of the War Years*

"James Tracy isn't merely a poet-philosopher or philosopher-poet; he's an architect who uses words to craft a vision of a new, better tomorrow. Then he takes to the streets and builds it." —**Jarret Lovell**, author of *Crimes of Dissent*

"James Tracy is one of the best public speakers I ever heard. His exquisite speaking skills are matched only by his remarkable and passionate writing about hidden moments of our history." —**Andrej Grubačić**, co-author of *Wobblies and Zapatistas*

"James Tracy will wake up any audience—they will see their tired assumptions blow away, and be better, happier, and stronger for it." —**Diane di Prima**

# DISPATCHES AGAINST DISPLACEMENT
Field Notes from San Francisco's Housing Wars

by James Tracy

AK PRESS
EDINBURGH · OAKLAND · BALTIMORE

*Dispatches Against Displacement: Field Notes from San Francisco's Housing Wars*
© 2014 James Tracy
Foreword © 2014 Willie Baptist

This edition © 2014 AK Press (Oakland, Edinburgh, Baltimore).
ISBN: 978-1-84935-205-5 | eBook ISBN: 978-1-84935-206-2
Library of Congress Control Number: 2014940774


AK Press                          AK Press
674-A 23rd Street                 PO Box 12766
Oakland, CA 94612                 Edinburgh EH8 9YE
USA                               Scotland
www.akpress.org                   www.akuk.com
akpress@akpress.org               ak@akedin.demon.co.uk

The above addresses would be delighted to provide you with the latest AK Press
distribution catalog, which features the several thousand books, pamphlets, zines,
audio and video products, and stylish apparel published and/or distributed by AK
Press. Alternatively, visit our websites for the complete catalog, latest news, and
secure ordering.

Cover design by Kate Khatib | manifestor.org/design
Photo spread curated by James Tracy and Fernando Martí.
Printed in the USA on acid-free paper.

**Dedicated** to the memories of Jazzie Collins, Howard Grayson, David McGuire, Al Thompson, Bill Sorro, and Rene Cazanave. The San Francisco Bay Area has indeed lost some of its finest fighters for the right to the city.

Welcoming my niece Evelyn Ball-Tracy to the world.

With love to Juliette Torrez, whose encouragement and insight makes me a better writer and person.

# Table of Contents

# Foreword
## by Willie Baptist

In *Dispatches Against Displacement: Field Notes from San Francisco's Housing Wars*, James Tracy speaks to the heart of the long-heralded American Dream: a home. This, along with other basic economic necessities, was articulated in the founding creed of this country in the expression of our rights to life, liberty, and the pursuit of happiness—that is, the human right to a house, not a shack, not a shelter, not a street corner. This notion has evolved over history and has become internationally recognized in the United Nations Universal Declaration of Human Rights, particularly in its article 25, which affirms the right to a decent standard of living and health.

The matter of housing is very close to me, as I have lived a life of poverty and have spent time on the streets of Philadelphia, Pennsylvania, homeless. Moreover, my involvement in the National Organizing Drive of the National Union of the Homeless in the late 1980s and early 1990s made me ever more sensitive to this critical issue. Currently, as a coordinator and educator of the Poverty Initiative at Union Theological Seminary and the Kairos Center for Religions, Rights, and Social Justice, I have reflected analytically on the injustices of poverty and homelessness as the defining problems of our times. To paraphrase Mahatma Gandhi, poverty is the worst form of violence and a violation of human rights. The worldwide housing and homelessness crises are particularly cruel and extreme manifestations of poverty, especially when we are living in a time of plenty. Indeed, poverty today is unnecessarily expanding and mass abandonment of homes is inhumanely and insanely existing next to an unprecedented and accumulating abundance for the very few. So I have come to understand the absolute urgency and necessity for this problem to be further studied and the solution to be found and fought for.

*Dispatches Against Displacement: Field Notes from San Francisco's Housing Wars* contributes to this central and indispensable discussion and fight.

Importantly, and as expressed in the insightful Herbert Marcuse quote that opens this book: "The housing crisis doesn't exist because the system isn't working. It exists because that's the way the system works." Mr. Tracy goes on to describe some of the features of the newly globalizing and urbanizing economic system that is at the same time an exploitative system for the many that concentrates wealth and resources for the few. This poverty-producing system is both life-threatening and life-taking, and it is turning the American Dream into a globalized nightmare with increasing mass evictions and homelessness. Today, the continuing stagnation and devastation of the 2007–8 economic crisis clearly reveals that this globalized crisis is more than cyclical. It is chronic and it is now displacing and pushing sections of the so-called "middle class" into impoverishment.

This book speaks to the fact that these worsening conditions are multiplying the ranks of the poor and dispossessed, compelling them to unite and fight for their very survival around a common basis of unity: the demand for the human right to housing and other basic economic necessities of life. It also raises to the fore some of the specific means by which the rich and power-wielding few manipulate the historically evolved racial divisions, particularly in the United States, as well as neoliberal and "Neo-Keynesian" policies to pre-empt and prevent this unity.

Mr. Tracy not only speaks of the plight but also the fight to abolish all poverty and homelessness, a growing global fight of the poor and evicted, which he has joined and to which he is himself committed. He writes about his organizing experiences and, along with his analysis of those experiences, he draws from the wisdom of other leaders of the housing and anti-poverty struggles, offering a number of strategic and tactical lessons for today's struggle. Tracy provides timely insight into the inescapable reality that looms ahead as the current global housing crisis and the worldwide economic crisis continue to worsen. It is important reading for anyone committed to fighting today's crises and building a new possibility of life, liberty, and happiness.

## Introduction: Of Delivery Trucks & Landlord Pickets

I DREAM'D in a dream,
I saw a city invincible to the attacks of the whole of the rest of the earth;
I dream'd that was the new City of Friends.
—Walt Whitman

The housing crisis doesn't exist because the system isn't working. It exists because that's the way the system works.
—Herbert Marcuse

First, a disclaimer: this is a partisan book. With the exceptions of the histories that occurred long before I was born, I was either directly in the fray or close by as events unfolded. In order for this book to be useful, I've had to turn a critical eye on people, organizations, and movements near and dear to my heart. This should be read as an organizer's notebook rather than a comprehensive history of the housing fights in San Francisco. Books brimming with New Urbanism's quixotic detachment can be found to the left and the right of this one on the shelves of your local bookstore. My urbanism is steeped in the politics of the human right of housing, to the city.

What do I want for the people whose stories populate this book? I want them to win.

In 1992, I drove a delivery truck for a thrift store in San Francisco's Mission District. I'd loved San Francisco from afar for years, growing up half an hour north. On a typical day, we could pick up a sofa in the Bayview District bric-a-brac on Potrero Hill, and then steal a long lunch staring into the Pacific Ocean. We didn't just learn how San Francisco's neighborhoods connected or where to get the best cheap Chinese food or Russian perogies; we were let in on a secret: the mythical San Francisco, the tolerant land of opportunity and wonder, was about to burst at the seams.

In every neighborhood, we received curious donations: the abandoned belongings of the evicted. This was just prior to the official acknowledgement that San Francisco was entering a housing crisis, yet all of the indications were in the back of our truck. The wardrobe left behind by an elderly woman in the Richmond. Children's toys in the Mission. Occasionally, the landlord would brag about the ouster. One told us, "It took me four months to get them out because of rent control."

"Where did they go?" I asked.

"Oh, there's plenty of public housing. I'm sure they will do fine," he replied.

My co-worker John, who was a little older than I was, was a confirmed socialist. He had quite a reputation as the kind of guy who would show up, newspaper in hand at a rally and denounce everyone around for being soft on capitalism. I never saw this side of him. When we talked about what we were seeing on the job, he would encourage me to read about the unemployed workers' movements of the Great Depression, where thousands of neighbors militantly defended each other from eviction. He convinced me to read Engels's "The Housing Question."[1]

My activist feet had been wet since high school, politicized through a combination of punk rock, fear of nuclear weapons, and an aborted Nazi skinhead invasion of my hometown. Because of what we saw every day on the job, right to housing stuck in my gut. On the truck I came up with a plan: we would organize tenant councils around specific evictions happening in their buildings or neighborhoods. These tenant councils would form a network, which would then work in solidarity with others for the long-term. The Eviction Defense Network (EDN) was born.

Because I was young, I was certain that no one in San Francisco besides our young organization knew what was to be done. In my mind at the time, the existing tenant rights community was too fixated on electoral fights to be of much use. I believed that affordable housing providers simply compromised politically. (Today, from the vantage point of a nonprofit job, I'm fully aware of my self-righteousness and lack of nuance.)

The EDN played an important role in San Francisco for a while. We were relentlessly independent. Funding a small office and phone with "Rock Against Rent" benefits at a local bar allowed us a degree of autonomy not granted to city-funded organizations. If your grandmother were being evicted, we'd go picket her landlord's home. If a person with AIDS were being tossed out, we'd find the landlord's business and shut it down. We were a pain in the ass and proud of it. We never succeeded in building the type of tenant syndicalism we envisioned, but our actions had an impact. Often, the extra pressure would prevent an eviction or at least leverage relocation efforts. When the landlords managed to place a rent control repeal on the ballot, we even ditched our dogmatic stance on electoral politics and joined with others in the tenant movement and helped beat it back by a big majority.

Because of our independence and chutzpah, eventually tenants of public housing reached out for us to join them in their corner of the housing crisis. Their problems were much different than that of the tenants in the private market who we were already working with. Instead of being pushed out solely for private profits, these tenants were caught up in an intricate web of privatization and structural racism. The Clinton administration (as you will read in Chapter 1) decided that the way to deal with public housing's problems was with a wrecking ball. A typical plan would preclude most of the tenants from returning.

As I got to know the community of North Beach public housing, I learned from them the history of the "other" San Francisco. In 1942, southern black workers were recruited to work in World War II industries in the Bay Area. In San Francisco they settled in the Fillmore District, housed in the homes of Japanese people interned after President Roosevelt signed Executive Order 9066 following the attack on Pearl Harbor. Post-war, the Fillmore thrived with black small businesses, jazz clubs, and a strong community. However, this too was not allowed to stand.

The Urban Renewal Act of 1949 allowed local governments to create redevelopment agencies that were able to seize private property through powers of eminent domain. All that was needed was the declaration that a neighborhood was blighted. The fact that the Fillmore had very little blight did not deter the San Francisco Housing Authority from a demolition rampage that displaced over 17,000 residents.

As an outsider, it was impossible to effectively organize alongside public housing residents without understanding the generational impacts of displacement. It would have been easy for me to frame the crisis in terms of cold public policy or my radical utopian aspirations. But for the people I was working with, displacement was just part of a long history of racism and to some minds a genocidal master plan.[2]

This experience changed me, turning me into the type of urbanist I am today. At the beginning, I didn't understand the finer contours of institutional racism. If I ever fixate too much on the impacts of white supremacy in the city, it's because of the stories tenants shared of regular displacement and discrimination.

My love of cities is untarnished and still a little romantic. The city is a place where people from all over the world are concentrated and have the potential to meet and make common cause. Seeing the twin engines of displacement through the market with that of the state has made me extremely leery of complete reliance on either as the only solution for the urban crisis. Today, despite many dozens of well-fought campaigns, San Francisco is even more exclusive and expensive. A modest two-bedroom apartment rents for about $4,000. The city as it is developed and redeveloped bears little resemblance to elected officials' rhetoric about a sharing economy.[3]

Cities simultaneously and effortlessly embrace both utopian and dystopian potentials. Most of them were born from human-caused ecological disasters—the clear cutting of forests, the paving of rivers and creeks. Today, the solutions to climate change are in part urban. Density can prevent sprawl and robust public transportation is the best way to cleave drivers from private automobiles. Through zoning and redlining, the political economy of cities has always been shaped by racism and white supremacy. It is in cities where oppressed people most often find each other, demand self-determination, and often forge coalitions. Dour, alienated architecture argues with vibrant design. Cities offer up the worst that popular culture can conjure and also give birth to rebel music such as hip-hop and punk, which in turn become the mass culture of another decade. Displacement replaces radical potential with spectacle. It is the change that kills off all other positive changes.

It doesn't really matter if one likes or dislikes cities. In 2008, for the first time, the percentage of the world's population living in cities outpaced those living in rural areas, and that population is likely to grow for the next few decades.[4] This makes questions about who governs, lives in, and is excluded from cities all the more critical to those who wish to chart a course for a more egalitarian world.

Throughout this book, I use the word "displacement" instead of "gentrification" in order to emphasize the result of uncontrolled property speculation and the impacts this process has on everyday people. The definition of "gentrification" in the Merriam-Webster dictionary is precise enough: *the process of renewal and rebuilding accompanying the influx of middle-class or affluent people into deteriorating areas that often displaces poorer residents.* However, the way the term is *used* often lacks the same precision. It is not uncommon to hear, as one liberal San Francisco supervisor opined, "A little gentrification is a good thing." Worlds of contradictions live within this deceptively simple sentence. What is usually meant is that neighborhoods need certain things, like grocery stores and basic infrastructure, to be whole, and that speaker can imagine only the arrival of affluent newcomers as the catalyst for this. It assumes that gentrification is as natural as granola, instead of a deliberate real estate strategy. Let's assume then that at least some of the people who profess to want gentrification really simply want a thriving neighborhood sans displacement. The final chapter, "Toward an Alternative Urbanism," offers some ideas about how to fight for development without displacement.

What to do now that cities are not feared in the way that they were fifty years ago? Politicians and pundits frame displacement as either an unfortunate side effect of urban progress or—in unguarded moments—a welcome cleansing. But it doesn't have to be this way; cities can grow, change, and welcome new citizens without running roughshod over the existing population. It is a mistake to frame anti-displacement politics as anti-change. After all, change is one of the things that made cities interesting places to live in the first place. Immigrants fleeing Latin American death squads and poverty represented change in the Mission District. The difference then was that the old-school Irish, Italian, and Jewish residents did not leave the neighborhood under the duress of an eviction notice. Working-class blacks who arrived in cities during the southern diaspora not only contributed their labor but also helped develop a strong urban cultural life. Those who come to a city fleeing homophobia, wanting to start a band, or to go to school are exactly what a good city is built upon. How then have monoculture and commodity come to dominate?

If the working-class spine of a city is broken, then no one but the moneyed get to dream big dreams in the city.

These dispatches defend the communities that make cities an amazing place to live: the working classes, artists, immigrants, and communities of color. They also make two modest proposals: first, that extending to the excluded the right to the city benefits all, and second, that excluded people can be active participants in building better cities, not just passive beneficiaries of progressive social policies.

The idea of the "right to the city" stems from the writings of Henri Lefebvre, an unorthodox Marxist who proposed that cities were the primary sites of contestation between capital and working-class movements.[5] This came as a bit of a shock to his contemporaries, who prioritized struggle at the point of production, such as factories. Today, with so few factories left in "First World" cities, Lefebvre's work is nothing short of prophetic. Alongside the conflicts over the production of goods, cities are also the sites of clashes over the production of *space* (campaigns against luxury housing and for neighborhood protections), *services* (domestic and fast food workers), and *human rights* (immigrant rights, school-to-prison pipeline organizing). Central to the idea is that "everyone, particularly the disenfranchised, not only has a right to the city, but as inhabitants, have a right to shape it, design it, and operationalize an urban human rights agenda."[6] Thanks to their direct engagement with grassroots organizations, Lefebvre's intellectual descendants have had an enormous influence on contemporary urban organizing; thinkers such David Harvey, Peter Marcuse, and Harmony Goldberg have been central to popularizing, updating, critiquing, and challenging Lefbvre's vision.

Today, the right to the city has truly never been further away from reality. Every year, the National Housing Law Project (NHLP) produces *Out of Reach*, a survey of housing costs, unique because of its emphasis on the links between wages and housing. Its methodology is based on what an average worker must make in order to afford a two-bedroom apartment, a figure they call the Housing Wage. The report has consistently shown that rents far outpace the means to pay not only in high-investment, hyper-gentrified cities like San

Francisco, but also in shrinking cities such as Detroit. In 2014, the national Housing Wage is $18.92 per hour, which means there is no state in the entire United States where a typical low-income worker can afford a two-bedroom apartment. San Francisco's Housing Wage is $37.62, almost four times the municipal minimum hourly wage of $10.74. If current campaigns to raise the minimum wage to $15 prevail, the wage-to-rent gap will still render most housing in the private market out of reach for many.[7]

Perhaps the moment when one becomes a political radical is the day one stops blaming all of the two-bit players for the problem and starts hating the game. Some of the individual landlords the EDN protested weren't just greedy, they were a cog in a much more complex urban machine—though I still don't have a problem with camping outside of a mansion to bring the crisis of displacement to the doorstep of a landlord. The system of real estate practiced in the United States in a dismal one, a cocktail of some of the worst features of serfdom and feudalism. Some of the landlords we pestered were small potatoes—part of the sandwich generation who had to simultaneously take care of parents and children. They bought rental property when it was cheap and they had decent jobs and wanted to cash in on their investment. With the money flooding in from the first dot.com rush, it was hard for small property owners not to. Some didn't feel like they had a choice. The profits represented college tuitions for their kids, an early retirement, health care and elder care. It was the real estate industry that relentlessly marketed San Francisco as the new frontier.

It wasn't uncommon for advertisements to read, "Be a pioneer in the former Wild West of the Mission District," or, "Up and coming neighborhood ready for a new sheriff in town." As someone who moved sofas for the minimum wage, I couldn't understand how in hot hell I could be part of the gentrification problem. But just as pioneers were manipulated by robber barons to clear the West, the presence of non-affluent artists, politicos, and punk rockers was needed to soften up the neighborhood.

Beyond the presence of the tattooed and the restless, there was something else going on: it was neoliberalism, something that my generation of activists associated with Chiapas or Bolivia but rarely connected to the home front.

In 1999, the American Friends Service Committee asked me to travel to Seattle to cover the WTO protests for their magazine *Street Spirit*. Thanks in part to the Zapatistas, the term "neoliberalism" was on everyone's tongue. I struggled with this; I thought it was strange that so many people who wanted to change the world ignored what was going on in their own backyards. After all, if neoliberalism was simply capitalism with the happy face torn off, weren't there plenty of signs of it in San Francisco?

"Neoliberalism" is one of the most abused terms in the political lexicon. Like "fascism," it is hurled as an epithet against any form of disagreeable political or economic activity. Simply put, neoliberalism is both an ideology and an economic strategy aimed at deregulating corporations, removing barriers to trade and commerce, and privatizing public resources. Commonly associated with international trade, neoliberalism has found a second home domestically, imbedding itself in the governance of major American cities.

San Francisco's economy has often been held hostage by neoliberal thinking, in turn fueling displacement and causing economic well-being and cultural diversity of communities to suffer. In 2001, fifty-two corporations sued the city of San Francisco over a dual payroll–gross receipts tax. The Board of Supervisors, fearing that the suit would bankrupt the city, voted to approve an $80 million settlement. The city paid for this by selling general obligation bonds—meaning that it sucked close to $100 million dollars out of the city coffers in tough economic times. The subsequent years were marked by severe budget cuts to housing, health care, and other essential services.

It would be a mistake, though, to say that the corporate agenda has ruled San Francisco without challenge and compromise. Grassroots organizing has extended workers' rights and protections to non-unionized service workers through municipal minimum wage and anti-wage-theft ordinances. The city boasts 26,000 units of permanently affordable housing. San Francisco even has its own form of universal health coverage for its residents, regardless of formal citizenship or ability to pay. And, despite the best efforts of the landlord lobby, rent control still offers basic protections for renters who live in buildings built before 1979.[8]

Yet the fact that San Francisco is even more exclusive and expensive can be traced directly to the embrace of neoliberalism in a progressive city. In 2011, the San Francisco Board of Supervisors granted a tax holiday to Twitter, Inc., the micro-blogging and social networking company founded in the city. Twitter threatened to move south to neighboring Brisbane unless its municipal payroll taxes were forgiven. Local politicians responded not only by granting a $22 million dollar tax break but by also approving a plan that has contributed to displacement citywide. At the time of the tax break, the deal was valued at between $4 billion and $6 billion.

Initial legislation proposed by Mayor Ed Lee would have given Twitter a complete payroll tax break in exchange for sticking around. Modified legislation, which passed, put forward by Supervisor Jane Kim, granted a six-year payroll exemption only for new hires and created an "enterprise zone" (including Twitter's new digs) on struggling Market Street and in parts of the Tenderloin and South of Market neighborhoods. The tax break extended to all businesses starting up in, or relocating to, the zone.

The enterprise zone economic development strategy grants corporations tax breaks and other advantages in exchange for doing business in an economically downtrodden neighborhood. Even though it is a conservative approach, based on incentives, most enterprise zones at least require the beneficiary businesses to commit to certain levels of local hiring and other community benefits. One problem is that after four decades of existence, they have shown little positive impact. According to the Public Policy Institute of California, employment rates within enterprise zones are no different than similar areas outside of them.[9]

The Twitter agreement didn't secure any benefits in a specific, legally binding manner. Tech companies have been widely criticized for promoting media stunts such as community cleanup days in place of grassroots economic development initiatives. Steve Woo, a community organizer with the Tenderloin Neighborhood Development Corporation, remarked, "The enterprise zone in the middle of Market Street was created by city officials without any specific commitment of addressing [the community's] needs and instead prioritized the needs of Big Business."

Even a progressive official such as Kim, who described herself as philosophically against such tax breaks, felt that she had to do business with Twitter. She pointed out in a public hearing that, without the legislation, all of the revenue from Twitter's payroll tax would leave San Francisco for the suburbs, and four hundred jobs would disappear from the local economy. Three years later, the tax break has cost the city $56 million. Advocates for the legislation pointed to the boarded-up storefronts on Market Street, and to the "seediness" of the area, claiming it was ripe for renewal. Kim was right—the choice to grant tax breaks was one choice among many that were all nearly as bad. It is a shining example that neoliberalism isn't just an economic strategy but also works to narrow what people see as possible options. After all, progressives hadn't put forward their own plan to breath life into boarded-up Market Street—it's no surprise that new money allied with old corporate property owners and built a coalition to reap massive profits with little thought to community impact.

Other community voices, such as the South of Market Community Action Network (SOMCAN), cited fears of displacement from a second dot-com economic boom. Neighborhoods bordering the "Twitter Zone" are largely working class and consist predominantly of renters. Supporters of the zone pointed out that these neighborhoods were in need of jobs and uplift and argued that because of decades of progressive zoning changes the neighborhoods were immune to gentrification.

The Twitter tax break has proved that many of the community's fears are correct. A non-subsidized one-bedroom apartment in the neighboring South of Market area starts at about $2,800 and can rent for as much as $8,000 a month. Angelica Cabande of SOMCAN, who led the attempt to defeat the Twitter tax break, explained, "City and state officials have been preaching that everyone needs to buckle down and make responsible decisions and make due sacrifices for the betterment of everyone; it doesn't make sense that big companies like Twitter get a tax break." Such is the dilemma facing politicians and policy makers. Employers like Twitter are able to move their offices much more easily than factories and plants did in the past, and this, combined with the current dearth of large employers, leaves cities hostage to corporate demands. It's the neoliberal economic model applied to local neighborhoods.

Twitter's economic blackmail has started a trend. Even before the ink had dried on this deal, another company, Zynga.com, delivered a demand of its own: stop taxing stock options, they told the city. Again the Board of Supervisors and the mayor obliged. What this is may be as simple as the politics of a hostage situation: give us the money or we'll kill the jobs. As you will read, the neoliberal fingerprints are also found all over the demolition of public housing and the weakening of rent control protections.

## Looking for the North Star: Radical Community Organizing in the 1990s Bay Area

When I first started organizing, many veteran activists took it upon themselves to buy me a copy of Saul Alinsky's *Rules for Radicals*. At one point, I had about a dozen copies on my bookshelf, all of which remained unopened until the latter part of the decade. Although community organizing had been going on in the United States since the first Native uprising, Alinsky, a brilliant and cantankerous Jewish man from Chicago, was often portrayed as its "godfather." In the early 1990s, several authors and organizers were starting to question Alinsky's large footprint on social justice work, pointing out a conflicted history of racial justice as well as an economy that was shifting from surplus to austerity.[10]

What Alinsky contributed was a coherent model, a set of tactics and strategies that were appropriate to large portions of America's working and middle classes in post-WWII America. He was not ambivalent about the need to shift power away from what today's activists call the 1 percent toward the 99 percent. Alinsky upheld that conflict, embodied in creative direct action, was essential in empowering the powerless.[11] He advocated permanent organizations, rooted in neighborhoods. He wasn't a Leninist and despised authoritarian versions of socialism. He believed that economic inequality within capitalism would always destroy the potential for freedom. In that sense, he would have been a logical grandfather for a new generation of anti-authoritarian organizers.[12] The fact that so many of the organizations that still upheld Alinsky seemed to be tied to the Democratic Party prevented us from a serious study of his ideas.[13]

He was a complex thinker, and I encourage anyone whose understanding of Alinsky stems from either right-wing Obama conspiracy theories or left-wing diatribes to get to know him in his own words. Alinsky was firmly a man of the progressive left and would have been saddened to know that people who wanted to reinforce the privileges of the already intensely privileged used his teachings.[14]

Alinsky believed that the United States held unlimited potential for deep democracy. He was a patriot who encouraged organizers to build on beliefs and traditions of the people they organize and situate their stories within American democratic traditions. This would later put him at odds with those radical organizers inspired by Third World revolutions, who had arrived at the conclusion that the United States was an unreformable and oppressive power, corrupt to the core. When considering Alinsky's importance today, it is more useful to focus on the challenges he posed to organizers, rather than on some of his own flawed conclusions. What forms of radicalism can everyday people actually relate to? How do you organize in a country where most workers identify with, or aspire to be part of, the middle class?[15]

Much has been written about Alinsky's struggles with organizing in the context of racialized capitalism. It's worth exploring this in order to gain an understanding of why so many activists of my generation discounted his importance—and also to complicate simplistic interpretations of his chauvinism. Alinsky's signature organizing project was in Chicago's Back of the Yards neighborhood, the one made famous by Upton Sinclair's novel, *The Jungle*.[16] The neighborhood council he created, the Back of the Yards Neighborhood Council (BYNC), helped to transform a beaten down area into a healthier (white) working-class area with improved housing, social services, and improved conditions in the neighborhood's warehouses.

Alinsky's critics point out that his reluctance to face race with working-class whites allowed the virus of white supremacy to fester. Alinsky's friend and biographer Nicholas Von Hoffman commented on the irony that BYNC's motto was "We the people will determine our own destiny," and that destiny was purely white.[17] The same community organizing skills used to improve the neighborhood could be employed in the service of reactionary racism. This pointed to one of the limits of the Alinsky model, which was dependent on winning the favor of established institutions like churches and unions. If these institutions were contaminated with racism, so would be the community organization they supported.

Alinsky hated this state of affairs but was ultimately caught inside the box of his own framework. Too much of what we now call popular education integrated into organizing struck him as patronizing—too similar to the ideologically rigid methods of the Communist Party USA.[18] He honestly believed that organized people would ultimately make the best decisions. This is can be true in many instances, but white supremacy proved itself to be a durable project. Groups such as the Center for Third World Organizing were pivotal in advancing the critique of Alinsky-inspired organizations and making a space for organizers of color to advance their leadership.

If not Alinsky, then what?

Many of the most committed organizers of the 1960s and 1970s had formed the "New Communist Movement" (NCM), which attempted to build the conditions for a Marxist-Leninist party to emerge and guide the nation toward a revolutionary overthrow of the government and capitalism. The character of NCM organizations varied greatly, from earnest working revolutionaries to cult-of-personality demagogues. What united most groups were roots in the 1960s civil rights, anti-war, and student struggles, an analysis that US imperialism was the enemy, and animosity to the idea of "reformism."[19] Throughout the Reagan years, many of these organizations kept left organizing alive through participation in workplace struggles, anti-apartheid organizing, and work against US intervention in Central and South America.

Many of us had contact with these organizers, but ran shrieking at the possibility of actually becoming cadre—for both good and bad reasons. We weren't stupid enough to believe that criticism of existing forms of communism were simply capitalist propaganda. As young rebels, we questioned the need for secretive and hierarchical leadership forms empowering a small group of leaders. At least in the beginning of our political involvement, my generation of organizers lacked the ideological compass that our predecessors possessed. We knew what we were against but had a hard time articulating what we were for. Were we for radical inclusion or a revolution? In some cases, our ambiguity allowed for a positive experimental approach to organizing, far more accountable to the people we were working with than the vague and mutable ideas of a future revolution. It equipped us for the type of organizing rooted in the politics of door-by-door, face-to-face conversations. It also left us in times of crisis trying to guide a ship without a rudder, ill equipped to answer many of the important questions arising in our work, such as the role of the state and the place of reform in the larger picture of social change.[20] Even if we initially lacked a grand unifying theory of social change, my generation of activists had strong international, national, and local influences on our ideas of social justice, starting in the decade in which we came of age—the 1980s.

During the Reagan years, many of the most catalyzing political movements were communicated through the lens of identity politics—battles against racism and homophobia, and for reproductive rights. Campaigns against US intervention in Latin America and in support of South Africa's apartheid regime also brought many into activism.

As Black South Africans fought to end racial apartheid, the international movement toward boycotts, divestment, and sanctions captured the imagination of many around the world, especially those in the San Francisco Bay Area. This solidarity movement was at its best when it drew connections between local and international racism. It also revealed the complicity of the United States in upholding apartheid, and at the same time provided ample opportunities for local action. Department stores selling South African gold krugerrands were protested, and the International Longshore and Warehouse Union refused to unload South African cargo imports. Organizing against apartheid put the conversation about race in the center of our emerging worldviews. Groups such as Anti-Racist Action, Red and Anarchist Skinheads, and others militantly confronted a resurgent white nationalist movement exemplified by White Aryan Resistance, Stormfront, and various smaller neo-Nazi groups, reminding many that the United States had not yet awakened from its own racial nightmare.

At that time, the religious right also began its own form of civil disobedience, through blockades at women's health clinics. The Clinic Defense (or Clinic Escort) movement brought forth a new generation of pro-feminist, pro-choice, pro–direct action activists.

Solidarity work confronting US military intervention was front and center in the 1980s and 1990s. Groups such as Committee in Support of the People of El Salvador and the Nicaraguan Institute for Community Action regularly sent delegations to Latin America in hopes that "brigadistas" would build an anti-imperialist movement upon their return to the States. These efforts were often the beginning of political consciousness for young North Americans. Related to this was the Sanctuary Movement, a mostly faith-based Underground Railroad for refugees of US proxy wars in the Central America.[21]

The emergence of the AIDS Coalition to Unleash Power (ACT-UP) and Queer Nation revitalized queer politics, with a focus on nonviolent direct action methods. Growing up in the Bay Area, it was rare to not know someone who had contracted HIV/AIDS, and ACT-UP's uncompromising spirit inspired many.[22] Queer Nation also made an impact by insisting on visibility in the Bay Area's suburbs—holding kiss-ins at malls and sports events. Taken together, these big-picture movements helped shape the worldviews of those who would become involved with community organizing in the coming years.

The last decade of the twentieth century was turbulent from its beginning. In 1990, the first invasion of Iraq, under George Bush Senior, brought many thousands of people to the streets. America's racial tinderbox was ignited once again in 1992, when police offers involved in the beating of Rodney King, a black motorist, were acquitted, resulting in the Los Angeles rebellions. And once again, in 1992, color and hue became central to the activist conversation as indigenous organizers brought forth a series of colorful and often confrontational mobilizations on the 500th anniversary of Columbus's arrival in the "new" world. For those of us who were struggling to contextualize these upsurges within our own experiences, we arrived at conclusions strikingly similar to our 1960s counterparts: the system of imperialism had both external and internal expressions.

In 1994, Congress passed the North American Free Trade Agreement (NAFTA), the most visible critics of which were a group of revolutionaries in Chiapas, Mexico, who launched an armed occupation of seven Mexican towns to protest the actual and cultural genocide resulting from free trade. To say that the Zapatista Army of

National Liberation was inspiring to North American activists is an understatement. Their theory of "leadership through obedience" came with a set of powerful stories and narratives. The story of dogmatic revolutionaries going to the mountains to recruit indigenous people into a political party, only to have their own practice transformed seemed to at least temporarily address the problems we had at home between strict top-down organizations and the covertly hierarchical consensus-based organizing.[23] It never fully addressed the problem, serving more as an ethical benchmark than a replicable organizing model. When the EDN was invited to work with residents of public housing, many of us were convinced that we could simply emulate the Zapatistas. Like many before us, we took a great example from another land and attempted to apply it mechanically to our own situations. (Probably not what Subcomandante Marcos or Comandante Ramona had in mind.)[24]

The pitched protest movements confronting right-wing attacks on the inclusive social progress of the 1960s and '70s and international revolutionary movements inspired my generation of organizers. Those of us who chose to operate on the neighborhood level believed that we were in fact connecting the dots between the global and the local, confronting the impacts of the global economy, racism, and a rising right in the neighborhoods we lived and worked in.

Throughout my life, I've seen moments like this through the battles for home and public space. They are always fleeting, as are the tenuous alliances that bloom and wilt again. Neoliberalism has literally stolen the city from those who most contribute to its vibrancy. While things will never be (and maybe never should) be the same, resistance—not only capital—shapes urbanism.

# Chapter One
## Landgrabs & Lies: Public Housing at the Crossroads

Did you hear about the rose that grew from a crack in the concrete?
Proving nature's law is wrong, it learned to walk without having feet.
—Tupac Shakur

**Thanksgiving Morning, 2003.** At the intersection of 30th and Mission Streets, an odd assortment of humanity—even by San Francisco standards—gathered. Homeless families, most with strollers in tow, cautiously mingled with trade-union activists; college students tried out their Spanish on Latino day laborers; street punks checked out the nonprofit workers with a sneer that acknowledged, "I'll probably be you one day." The crowd of about 140 had diversity written all over it—they were old and young, with enough ethnicity to make even the most jaded observer speak about Rainbow Coalitions. Picket signs read "Let Us In!" The mood remained mellow, maybe strangely so for a crowd of people who, in an hour's time, would participate in an illegal occupation of vacant housing—just one vacant unit among thousands owned by the San Francisco Housing Authority (SFHA),[1] the troubled agency charged with providing homes for the city's most impoverished.[2]

The bus chartered to bring the protesters to the secret takeover site was late. The driver, reached by cell phone, reported a holiday hangover from which he'd just woken up. He would be stopping for a strong cup of coffee.

Even though it was Thanksgiving Day, there was more than one protest going on in San Francisco; a couple of hundred feet away, United Food and Commercial Workers members picketed Safeway in the ongoing battle over the company's attempts to decimate employee healthcare benefits. A delegation went over to wish the unionists well, as one nervous housing protester tried to conceal the Safeway logo on her fresh cup of coffee.

The press showed up early to search for a spokesperson, played today by Carrie Goodspeed, a formerly homeless twenty-four-year-old organizer with Family Rights and Dignity (FRD).[3] She's nervous at first but then relaxes. "The Authority [SFHA] owns over one thousand units of vacant housing that could be used to house families. We will risk arrest to make this point."

"Is this the right thing to do?" blurted out one reporter. There's silence, and the expression of someone having second thoughts crosses Godspeed's face. Suddenly that expression disappears.

"Definitely. It's the right thing to do."

Takeover! The caravan consisting of five autos, some bikes, and the long-awaited bus arrived at the tip of the West Point Housing Development. Banners in the windows proclaimed: "HOMES NOT JAILS FOR HOMELESS FAMILIES," and "THESE UNITS SIT VACANT WHILE FAMILIES SLEEP ON THE STREETS." The dwelling, at 45 Westpoint, was opened up the night before by a covert team. The strategy was for one group of people to do the breaking and another to do the entering, so as to shrink potential criminal charges.

Some were there to pressure the Authority to rehabilitate the vacant units. Homeless people added another thoroughly practical perspective: "If I get busted, I sleep inside. If I don't, I sleep inside," one person remarked.

In front of the building, a resident of the development, Camila Watson, took the microphone. Watson is one of the reasons this action landed here—because of her outreach most of the neighbors are reasonably supportive. When Watson became homeless, she turned for help to Bianca Henry of FRD, one of the women occupying the apartment. Watson's name had "disappeared" from the Housing Authority's waiting list. Extremely aggressive advocacy (oftentimes visiting at the Authority's offices to file a complaint with a bullhorn) had helped the agency "find" Watson and offer her a place to live.

"I used to come by here and think, 'Why can't I live in apartment 41, or 45, or 47? Give me paint and a hammer and I'll fix it up.'" With housing, other good things have come to pass. Watson now holds down a job, and is doing well at City College. The experience left her determined to fight for those still stuck in the shelter system.

"They say these units are vacant because people don't want to live here. I haven't met a mother yet that wouldn't move here over the streets and the shelter."

Another woman told a story of how her homelessness began the day the government demolished the public housing development where she lived and reneged on promises for replacement housing. One resident remarked that she feared taking homeless family members into her home, since her contract with the Authority made that act of compassion an evictable offense. A young poet named Puff spoke in a style that was equal parts poetry slam, evangelism, and comedy. By the end of her time on the microphone, she managed to connect homelessness, minimum-wage work, consumerism, police abuse, war, and genocide. The San Francisco Labor Chorus rallied the group in rousing renditions of post-revolutionary holiday favorites such as "Budget La-La-Land," stretched to fit "Winter Wonderland," and "Share the Dough," set to the tune of "Let It Snow."

As many neighbors stopped by, a trio of young men came down the hill. "Is that where the homeless people are going to live?" the tallest one asked.

"We hope so!" yelled Bianca Henry from the second floor window.

"How many rooms?"

"Three!" Henry replied.

The youngest looking of the three flashed a smile gleaming with gold caps, "Happy Thanksgiving, Yo!" as the trio continued down the hill.

## From Hope to Hopeless, The Local Politics of Austerity

> Within a very short time people who never before could get a decent roof over their heads will live here in reasonable comfort and healthful, worthwhile surroundings.
>
> —President Franklin Delano Roosevelt, at the opening of Atlanta's Techwood Homes 1940

How was it possible for thousands of units of public housing to sit vacant in the middle of a housing crisis? Life for the San Francisco Housing Authority, as San Francisco's largest landlord and last line of defense against homelessness, has never been easy. Born in 1940, the SFHA initially housed returning servicemen and their families.[4] Over the years, it grew to operate over 6,575 units of housing and administer another 10,000 units in conjunction with other partners. In the late 1980s, then-Secretary of Housing and Urban Development Jack Kemp announced the creation of the Housing Opportunities for People Everywhere (HOPE) program, which would tear down public housing and rebuild it. HOPE was intended to move the feds out of housing provision by transferring ownership to resident cooperatives. Kemp's cocktail was infused with doses of privatization and austerity, yet it wasn't a road map for displacement. Homes would have to be replaced on a one-to-one basis. It assumed and allowed for most residents to return. If the federal government, like a father in a divorce, left the house, it at least tried to leave it in good working order.

In 1990, the Cranston-Gonzalez Affordable Housing Act created HOPE VI, infusing new funding into the revitalization of public housing. In theory, the original tenants are able to return to their refurbished homes and enjoy a wide range of social and economic programs designed to ease the transition from welfare to work. Democratic president Bill Clinton removed most of the hope from the HOPE program when, in 1995, requirements for resident participation, return, and unit replacement were stricken from the federal record. Smaller developments meant that not every family even had a place to return. In reality, what often happened was that the reconstruction was delayed or abandoned altogether, or the "mixed income" residency requirements caused the poorest of the tenants—those most in need of subsidies—to lose their homes.

Since 1992, the US Department of Housing and Urban Development (HUD) has awarded 446 HOPE VI grants in 166 cities. A 2004 study found that only 21,000 units had been built to replace the 49,828 demolished units.[5] In other words, only 42 percent of the demolished public housing has been replaced. Other estimates put the loss higher, suggesting 50 percent of the public housing stock has been slashed.

No amount of "resident empowerment" can change the fact that once a building is finished, it will shortly suffer small and large injuries. When the elevator breaks or a pipe bursts it is usually too expensive for the residents—minimum-wage workers, senior citizens, and government-assistance recipients—to repair. To meet the deficit in operating costs, the SFHA requested proposals from both for-profit and nonprofit developers to redevelop its properties—again raising the specter of displacement—what would be dubbed "The Plan" by many residents, thanks to a shameful history of being on the receiving end of plans. Many residents, some who lived through the "urban removal" of the 1960s, saw the demolition as one more attempt to kick blacks out of town.

The term "urban removal" refers explicitly to the government-financed and -facilitated destruction of inner-city housing. In the case of HOPE VI, the destruction is of government-owned developments, but in some cases, the government also seized private property and removed entire communities.

Memories of landgrabs past are hard to erase. The word on the street accused then-Housing Authority Executive Director Ronnie Davis of giving his staff free rein to evict outspoken tenants, forge documents, and take bribes. Davis was never convicted of any wrongdoing while in San Francisco but was later convicted of embezzling from his former job—the Cayahuga Housing Authority in Cleveland, Ohio. High-ranking officials under Davis's watch in San Francisco were convicted of auctioning portable Section 8 vouchers to homeless families. One mother met the asking price by taking a loan from a local drug dealer, and ended up serving a short time on federal probation.[6]

### Tenants: Putting the Hope back into HOPE VI

From the beginning, residents of San Francisco's public housing and a handful of allies organized to put real hope back into the HOPE VI process. In 1995, an ad hoc group, Fillmore In Struggle Together (FIST), put the public housing issue on the map by mobilizing residents of Hayes Valley public housing to disrupt a conference of housing professionals gathering to discuss HOPE VI. Several officials expressed covert support for tenant activists by feeding FIST inside information about the Housing Authority's intention to displace residents.[7] In 1996, a small group of highly organized residents of North Beach public housing in San Francisco began to raise questions about the fate of their homes, slated to be demolished under HUD's HOPE VI program a few years later. Because two other Hope VI Projects in the city had remained vacant mud lots for two years, residents invited the San Francisco–based Eviction Defense Network (EDN), which had led a campaign to prevent the evictions of undocumented residents, to help organize others in the development. The residents and EDN began a slow process of door-to-door organizing.[8]

Residents at North Beach had their work cut out for them. Very basic demands, such as the right to return to their homes after redevelopment and the hiring of local residents in the construction process were dismissed by Housing Authority officials or given superficial and vague lip service. Resident leaders were well aware of the treatment that tenants of other Housing Authority and HUD sites had received for organizing. Across town at Geneva Towers, all but the two dozen or so activist residents had been successfully relocated, intransigence that was largely believed to be passive-aggressive retaliation. It took a sleep-in, led by tenant association president Louise Vaughn, on the front lawn of HUD Secretary Art Agnos to wrestle relocation vouchers for the remaining residents.[9] HOPE VI residents at Hayes Valley public housing revolted after the relocation process was accelerated and they were given just thirty days to find replacement housing. Valley residents were also shocked to discover that demolition plans were secretly approved by a former resident of their development, not an elected body as was then required by federal law.[10] At North Beach, residents found that a sign-in sheet for a community meeting had been cut-and-pasted into a petition asking HUD to demolish the property. The Housing Authority also routinely offered vocal tenants employment or vacated evictions in exchange for support of HOPE VI. North Beach tenant activist Bethola Harper explained the game: "We learned that we couldn't sign anything without it being used against us. We learned that agreements we made with the Housing Authority were meant to be broken as soon as they could demonstrate enough tenant support to satisfy HUD. Most importantly, we learned never to air out any differences in front of the city. If we had to argue, we needed to meet amongst ourselves to work out our own problems. They were always looking for ways to spread rumors and pit the races against each other. The end goal was to get as many of us out, and pay for as little relocation as possible."

Calling out the demolition machine was dangerous business. In 1994, former Black Panther Party member Malik Rahim was hired by the SFHA to assist in educating tenants at the Bernal Dwellings (aka Army Street) about their relocation options in the HOPE VI process. At the time of his hire, the agency knew full well about Rahim's radical past and five-year stint in prison for armed robbery. It only became a problem after he realized that the HOPE VI plan at Bernal would return as few as one-third of the original tenants. Rahim quit his job and started organizing tenants against the plan, calling meetings to build a greater tenant voice in the process and to demand the right to return. Defending public housing tenants was hardwired into Rahim's political outlook; residents of Desire Housing Projects had militantly defended the New Orleans Panthers—his chapter—from an attack by the police.[11]

Rahim allied with former Bernal resident Jeff Branner to organize the residents. During the 1980s, the Branner family controlled the majority of the crack trade at the development. He had served five years in prison, and there was no evidence that he had returned to the trade post-release. However, after leaving the Housing Authority's good graces, both men's pasts were fair game again. A newspaper article alleged that violent convicts had taken over the tenant association, followed by a three-day investigative series on a local television channel. The truth could have not been more mundane; the tenant association was hardly controlled by the two. However, many residents were indeed alarmed by Branner's return and had called the police to complain.

Shortly after the media flurry, the SFHA boarded up the tenant association's offices. Branner and Rahim broke into the room to retrieve personal belongings and outreach records and were arrested for trespassing. The two faced charges that could have resulted in long prison sentences due to past convictions, but those charges were dropped thanks to the work of legendary activist lawyer, William Kunstler, who was no stranger to defending Black Panthers. It was Kunstler's final case before his death in 1995. In a final attempt to put Branner away, police resurrected a 1993 cocaine possession charge. He pleaded guilty to possession but not to intent to sell. Under an unusual sentencing arrangement, he was sentenced to probation and 1,000 hours of community service for which he would advise the school district on gang-intervention strategies.

Organizing at North Beach was difficult but made easier by a group of dedicated tenant leaders, most of them with prior experience in organizing. One tenant leader, Gregory Richardson, had been active as a youth in fighting the destruction of the Western Addition. Alma Lark, a dynamic and cantankerous elder, did trench work in the Southern Christian Leadership Conference during the 1960s civil rights movement and was an associate of Ella J. Baker. Bethola Harper was a former member of the Black Panther Party. Other key leaders, such as Donald Hesbitt and Thomas Toy, had taken part in strikes as trade union members.

The partnership with the EDN worked in a variety of ways. One resident leader joked that the residents needed the outsiders because "the elevators are broken down and we're too old to go up and down the stairs doing outreach all the time. The [EDN] people are young and don't mind going up the stairs and doing some door-knocking."

At first, the tenant response was limited to mobilizing at hearings of the Board of Supervisors. As indiscriminate evictions picked up in pace, they also had to open up new fronts. "One Strike" raised the stakes in any negative encounter that a resident might have with the police, private security, or Housing Authority staff.[12] They asked the Coalition On Homelessness to train activist residents in the art of Cop Watching and to loan them the video cameras to do it with.[13] They designed stickers that read "Police and Thieves Watch Out: This is a Working-Class Neighborhood," alongside an icon of a VHS video camera. Since pubic relations is everything during a redevelopment process, the threat of being caught on videotape helped put the agency on notice and chilled out the behavior of their security forces.[14]

These evictions were part of a national policy shift, and were extremely effective in clearing residents out of HOPE VI sites. In 1996, President Clinton signed into law a bill designed to accelerate evictions in public housing. Dubbed "One Strike and You're Out," it was touted as a way to stop drug trafficking and violent crimes in public housing developments. Since One Strike was a civil procedure, tenants could be evicted even if they were acquitted of criminal charges. In effect, what One Strike did was provide an excuse for eviction based solely on innuendo and allegations of criminal activity. Housing authorities across the country evicted entire households based on the arrest of one member. In one case, a grandmother was brought to court after her grandson, whom she hadn't seen in several years, was arrested on drug possession charges in the neighboring county.

In another case, Housing Authority resident Zelma Matthews was evicted because of her son's drug charges. A Housing Authority document uncovered by one reporter, Angela Rowen, confirmed that One Strike would be used to help the agency conform to new "income-mixing requirements" by weeding out low-income tenants like Matthews.

The turning point in the campaign came in 1998, as residents and their allies looked for ways to escalate the fight. Some advocated for a non-violent blockade of one of San Francisco's fabled cable cars, which ironically ended its route in a plaza that cut through the development. As resident Patsy Brown recalled, "When the City decided to extend the cable car stop down a few blocks in the middle of the development, I had a feeling we would have to go sooner or later." The idea was eventually voted down in favor of a tenant speak-out because of concerns that tenant arrests might lead to evictions, and arrests of allies would signal that resistance to HOPE VI was only the work of outside agitators.

Together, the group came up with another option: they would go ahead and organize a rally but encourage residents to pledge not to move until a list of ten relocation and re-occupancy demands were met. Households displayed trilingual "Sign-the-Contract" window signs. Their ability to hold up the relocation process was the only leverage the tenants had. Federal requirements mandated strict time-tables, which meant that a coordinated refusal to move would jeopardize the funds needed to initiate the demolition. Activists knew it was a bluff and that the actual capacity to defend such an action was questionable. "We were brave, but we were often really scared. Housing [the SFHA] was always looking for ways to get us out. The slightest little mistake they would use against you—your kids being too loud, bad housekeeping, whatever. At the same time, we knew that we weren't going to get anywhere by doing nothing," remarked North Beach tenant activist Benita Grayson.

Racial tensions also flared up as the campaign went on. Nearly identical rumors about tenant leaders on the take or secretly signing off on each other's ouster abounded, initially splitting the Asian and African-American tenants. The source of these rumors was revealed to be Housing Authority staff themselves when one was caught spreading falsehoods—in Cantonese—to a Chinese tenant. This staff member was unaware that an African-American neighbor understood basic Cantonese. Armed with this information, the EDN convinced the different factions to sit down with each other, with adequate translation, to dispel any misconceptions the rumors had created. This led to over 60 percent of the tenants signing a pledge to not move until the exit contract was delivered with real guarantees. By and large, residents stood firm, refusing relocation at a time when the SFHA needed to begin the process to comply with HUD mandates. Fearing that a protracted battle could cause it to lose $23 million in HOPE VI money, the SFHA finally relented.[15]

The Housing Authority capitulated to some important demands. An "Exit Contract" contained legally binding guarantees, most significant among them one-for-one replacement of all demolished low-income units and a limited number of reasons that could disqualify one from re-occupancy. The SFHA executive director presented the signed contract on September 22, 1999, in front of the City Board of Supervisors' Finance and Labor Committee during a hearing around the Public Housing Tenant Protection Act (PHTPA).[16]

The HOPE VI program became part and parcel of the overall push toward privatizing resources once held for the public good. Far from bringing in needed resources, the trend has been to remove tenant protections and clear the way for more developer profit. For example, North Beach's new, private, for-profit management company tried to stipulate that it could convert vacated low-income units to market rate, even though all low-income units would be initially rebuilt. Remarkably, with the help of Housing Is a Human Right, another small organizing group, residents who by this time were relocated across the Bay Area returned to protest. This conversion plan was scrapped.

The partnership of tenants and outside organizers was especially strong in this campaign. The tenants brought to the table the dedication of people fighting for their future. The EDN brought with it a willingness to organize alongside tenant leaders, instead of usurping their power.

### This Town is Headed for a Ghost Town?

Back at 45 Westpoint, Ted Gullicksen, a co-founder of Homes Not Jails, takes the bullhorn. Speaking from the broken window, he invites the press and anyone else to check out the apartment. "It won't take thousands of dollars to fix it up."

Gullicksen, a working-class Bostonian, co-founded Homes Not Jails to add a direct action component to the San Francisco Tenants Union, which he directs. The group has several "survival squats," shorthand for covert squats meant to house people for as long as possible. In contrast, 45 Westpoint is a short-term "political squat" used to protest the housing crisis, popularize demands, and generally raise a ruckus. At a political squat, the occupiers don't expect to be staying for long. In fact, they may spend more time in county jail than in a reclaimed building.[17]

This ruckus is usually raised on major holidays, especially the very cold ones. San Francisco's press is usually quick to broadcast sensationalistic stories about homeless people using drugs or having mental health breakdowns in public places. Such "journalism" has played a major role in mustering public support for punitive anti-homeless legislation.[18] On takeover days, the camera is forced to observe pictures of homeless people at their most powerful, instead of their most vulnerable. Images of poor people and their allies repairing broken apartments replace myopic images of addiction. Homes Not Jails specializes in the strategic use of a slow news day. As Coalition On Homelessness co-founder Paul Boden remarked, "Homeless people have to be militant to even get a chance of being portrayed as human beings who are capable of organizing themselves, making decisions, and setting agendas. Even when we take bold actions like housing takeovers, the media is likely to portray us as people who are begging for a handout."[19]

What about the former residents of 45 Westpoint? What happened to them and who were they? The house holds a few clues. Stickers on the upstairs bedroom door read "Audrina loves Biz." Judging from the artifacts of the development, they were likely Black or Samoan. Large plastic "Little Tykes" toys left behind suggest a child, probably two. The only other evidence is a sewing machine, a conch shell, and a broken entertainment center.

What caused their exit? Did the family leave in response to the gang turf wars that periodically erupt on the hill? Were they recipients of a "One Strike" eviction?

Bianca Henry surveys the Thanksgiving rebellion with pride, a grin playing on her lips. For someone who was raised in the projects and knows firsthand the over-reaching arm of the law, the fact that she is purposely risking arrest for the cause is a small but dramatic personal revolution.

Henry's pride in her work is evident. Together with other parents, she has done one of the hardest things a community organizer can do: inspire poor people to move beyond "Case Management" and "Services" and take things to the next level: collective action. The action is separated into two zones: the Arrest Zone (inside the house) and the Safe Zone (on the grass outside). It assumes a social contract with the police to respect Arrest and Safe zones. Henry knows firsthand that even minor brushes with the law can bring the wrath of the CPS, INS, POs, PDs, and various other Big Brother–like institutions adept at tearing families apart.

Henry believes that if you want to get anything done, you can't just wait for the next election, though she can effortlessly rattle off obscure public-policy points and arcane aspects of the Code of Federal Regulations as they pertain to housing poor people. Starr Smith is Bianca's co-organizer. A white single mom who came to work with Family Rights when she was still homeless, she's on the outside fielding questions and dealing with the dozens of unforeseen snafus cropping up minute by minute. They make an interesting team. Henry grew up in the thick of gangs, and her neighborhood was devastated by the crack cocaine industry. She exemplifies the Tupac generation of young people who grew up in the era where every reform won during previous upheavals was being stripped away.[20] Smith came of age following the Grateful Dead in the final days of Jerry Garcia. In many ways the eclectic crowd is a reflection of this partnership.

Later in the afternoon, one neighbor the group forgot to outreach to is steaming pissed—the president of the tenant association.

She confers with Jim Williams, head of security of the SFHA, and insists that he call the police. Surprisingly, he doesn't seem too worried. Sarcastically he asks Jennifer Friedenbach of the Coalition on Homelessness to please call the agency when the protest is over.

"We're not leaving; we're moving more people in," Freidenbach answers.

"Yeah, right," Williams retorts.

"Really."

"Well… Why don't we have our legal people call yours?"

### Hope-Based Punishment

Like the Lucha Libre characters of Mexican wrestling, the Republican and Democratic parties have generally tag-teamed on dismantling the social support system ushered in by the New Deal. Throughout the 1990s, the rhetoric of welfare reform blamed "cultures of poverty" and "concentrations of poverty" for poverty itself. In other words, poverty can be blamed on bad parenting, low community expectations, and even poor people living too close to each other. These terms were popularized by right-wing politicians such as Newt Gingrich. In the 1990s this framework was used to obscure the roles of free trade agreements, structural unemployment, and the persistence of racism in perpetuating deep poverty. Residents of public housing were on the receiving end of a series of punitive measures that worked alongside the HOPE VI program to empty out federal housing.

Another Clinton-era gift, the Quality Housing and Work Responsibility Act (QHWRA) of 1998, mandated that all public housing developments should become "mixed income," usually meaning a reduction in homes available to very-low-income people. QHWRA also ripped housing subsidies from households of undocumented immigrants.

Urban land being at a premium, the HOPE VI process usually results in the privatization of many developments as developers contracted to do the reconstruction generally gain partial ownership of the new housing (currently estimated at around $1 billion). So the poor continue to lose, as corporations, such as McCormack Baron and Sun America, make immense profits.

Taken together, these measures accelerated spatial deconcentration—the exodus of low-income people of color from city centers to outlying suburbs. Spatial deconcentration has long been a staple in the pantheon of far-left (particularly anarchist) conspiracy theories. The theory went that, in response to the inner city uprisings (popularly known as riots) of the late 1960s and the threat of urban revolutionaries, the government set out to break up urban neighborhoods of color as a means of curtailing rebellion. It is alleged that an African-American federal worker, Yolanda Ward, was executed in the middle of Washington, DC, to prevent her from exposing the policy shift.[21]

Whether Ward was executed for this reason or not, it is no secret that spatial deconcentration remains the anchor of what remains of federal housing policy. The US Code of Federal Regulations identifies "the growth of population in metropolitan and other urban areas, and the concentration of persons of lower income in central cities," and sets a goal to "develop new centers of population growth and economic activity." Its objective is "the reduction of the isolation of income groups within communities and geographical areas and the promotion and increase in the diversity and vitality of neighborhoods through the spatial deconcentration of housing opportunities for persons of lower income and the revitalization of deteriorating neighborhoods."

A report by the Eviction Defense Collaborative (EDC), a legal aid organization, provides a sense of the link between deconcentration and displacement. By tracking their own clients, the EDC found that over half moved from San Francisco after an eviction. About a quarter could be contacted through a post office box, implying that the household had become homeless. Displaced residents generally are dispersed to the rim cities of Antioch, Vallejo, San Pablo, Dixon, El Cerrito, and Vacaville.[22] Some, like Vallejo and Concord, have suffered high unemployment rates as a result of military base closures. So public housing transplants to these areas often have to commute to the metropolitan areas to find low-wage work.[23] Housing Authority self-sufficiency experts also aggressively marketed homeownership to employed residents. Under this plan, residents were allowed to cash-out Section 8 vouchers for considerable down-payment assistance. Unfortunately, many were also ushered toward the same subprime lenders who would become the villains of the foreclosure scandal less than a decade later.

Overt political racism is another issue that refugees of displacement have to face in the rim cities. A case in point is the early morning raid conducted by a Vallejo city taskforce on the federally subsidized but privately owned Marina Green development in 1997. Over sixty families were rousted from their beds and forced to watch as officers ransacked their apartments.[24] The Vallejo Police Department selected which houses to raid based on membership on county welfare rolls.

The irony of federal housing policy "reform" is that it used a progressive critique to accomplish the completely conservative aims of privatization and austerity. The HOPE VI program argues against warehousing the poor in substandard areas, and many housing authorities actually have self-sufficiency programs for their residents to prepare for gainful employment. However, by cutting funding and abolishing the requirement that demolished public housing units be replaced on a one-for-one basis, Congress has effectively given the federal government an exit strategy from the public housing business.

## The Continuing Appeal of Voting with a Crowbar

More often than not, reliance on voting in periodic elections has sidetracked them from the more powerful weapons of direct action. By engaging in the continuous struggle for justice and human welfare, workers will gain a realistic political education and cast the only ballot worth casting—the daily ballot for freedom for all.
—Bayard Rustin "New South, Old Politics"


You talk about Africa, I laugh at ya. 'Cause things aren't too good here in America.
—N.W.A. "Fuck the Police"

The takeover of 45 Westpoint took place at a curious point in US activist history: when radicals, catalyzed by the global justice movement, chased trade summit after trade summit in cities such as

Seattle, Genoa, Geneva, and Washington, DC. The dialogue of direct action unearthed movement anxieties about race, class, and provenance at every turn. After all, as deserving of a drubbing as the World Trade Organization was, it took a fair amount of resources to follow them around the globe just to risk arrest. Elizabeth Betita Martinez wrote an influential essay entitled "Where Was the Color in Seattle?" Tragically, one never needs to ask that question about homeless shelters. In San Francisco, the Black population is at a dismal 6.5 percent, compared to over 48 percent of the Shelter system's population. The national statistics aren't much better. A recent report drawn from US Census data demonstrates that Black people are disproportionately represented in shelters by a nearly 3:1 margin.[25]

The Westpoint takeover exposed another urban reality: that solidarity in the city is possible. Though the city has a long catalog of problems, it is also a place where people of wildly different backgrounds met by necessity. Even in deeply segregated cities, the chance of such encounters are much more likely than in rural areas. Bus service may be unequal depending on the dominant hue of the neighborhood, but sooner or later we all transfer to the same bus, if only to exit shortly thereafter. Organizations like the Coalition on Homelessness recognize that their constituents, homeless families, are but one spoke in the wheel of urban citizenry. They had the option, and of course the right, to organize in isolation. Instead, they chose a path that dignified all parties. But there was ample space for others to take part without being reduced simply to the role of "ally."

This day took over a year's worth of preparation. The mostly white Homes Not Jails met regularly with Family Rights and Dignity at the offices of the Coalition on Homelessness. Through this process, meticulous plans were laid—everything from the art and science of sharing the media spotlight, to legal protections and childcare.

There has always been a dance between electoral politics and direct action, even if their partisans are uncomfortable with that fact. Direct action was central in the fights for the right to expand suffrage to women and later Blacks. The women of Family Rights and Dignity and the squatters of Homes Not Jails embody a spirit of past social movements, such as the unemployed workers of the 1930s, which is rooted in the everyday needs of community members. They build direct democracy with crowbars as their ballots and vacant housing as their ballot boxes. Nine years later, activists energized by the Occupy movement turned to exactly this style of organizing, confronting evictions and joblessness on the neighborhood level.

As an action initiated mostly by working-class women of color, the one at 45 Westpoint shows alliances can be built between America's different dissident factions. It begins with supporting self-organized actions such as this and respecting the fact that communities that find themselves under the boot of poverty need people to have their back—not to act as spokespeople for their cause. Despite displacement spasms, the city is still a place where people of disparate backgrounds can meet, find common grievances, and engage in common collective action.

45 Westpoint, and 225 other vacant homes, were opened to homeless families in February 2004.

### Postscript on a Demolition Rampage

> Now you can tear a building down but you can't erase a memory (Memory)
> These houses may look all run down but they have a value you can't see
> (You've got to fight, you've got to fight) Now you can tear a building down
> (You've got to fight for your neighbourhood) But you can't erase a memory
> —Living Colour, "Open Letter to a Landlord"

Scholars and public officials will likely be debating whether the HOPE VI program was a "success" or a "failure" for decades to come. The answer depends on how one defines the words. HOPE VI successfully followed a neoliberal playbook to slash public expenditures on the housing safety net and transfer part of the commons into private hands. Doing this required a set of assumptions leading to the conclusion that there was no alternative method of revitalizing public housing except for shrinking its footprint. HOPE VI relied on the same stereotypes of residents used in 1994's bipartisan welfare reform push and the Reagan-era "welfare queen" tropes. Early HOPE VI literature touted that the program would benefit poor people by putting them in contact with middle-income people and would "help low-income people acquire middle-class values and motivation to help break the cycle of poverty."[26] The presumption that poverty and pathology walked hand-in-hand was key to the HOPE VI public relations machine.

Not all HOPE VI projects were equally disastrous for tenants. In Seattle, all current residents were successfully relocated, although the overall stock of public housing was shrunk. In Pittsburgh, the HOPE VI process went forward with little displacement thanks in part to highly organized community organizations, strong community planning, and ample available land.

With and without HOPE VI, local housing authorities have pursued public housing demolitions with federal endorsement. In 2008, Representatives Barney Frank and Maxine Waters called for a moratorium on HUD approvals of new public housing demolition until a viable affordable housing strategy could be renewed. The demolition of Chicago's Cabrini-Green development replaced only 10 percent of the original homes. In post-Katrina New Orleans, city officials operating under the cover of the hurricane moved to demolish 4,500 homes. In 2007, police used tasers and stun guns against public housing residents demanding a voice at a City Hall meeting where the demolition was being rubber-stamped.[27]

In San Francisco, tenant activism forced the SFHA to alter its plans in several important ways, but the HOPE VI program still resulted in the loss of critical housing. The first three developments that were reconstructed contained 25 percent fewer units. Two developments, those with the most sustained and consistent tenant activism—Valencia Gardens and North Beach—were built with additional units. The SFHA has not tracked the fates of those pushed out in the HOPE VI process. At Valencia Gardens, only five families that lived in the development pre-demolition remain as of 2014.[28] Today, the exit contract won by the North Beach Tenant Association is the base level of protections for planned public housing renovations, thanks to the organizing of the Housing Rights Committee which finally won a Public Housing Tenant Protection Act in 2011.[29]

The most tragic part of HOPE VI is that it was a perfect example of how ideology stole an opportunity to put a meaningful dent in national poverty. The majority of the alternatives were not complicated or even very expensive. First, Congress could have easily maintained the one-for-one replacement requirements jettisoned in 1995 and guaranteed all residents the right to return. The influx of many millions of dollars of public money should have been used in an aggressive jobs program giving residents the chance to advance in the trades, as well as access to post-construction job opportunities. Perhaps the only truly political daunting task would have been to finally crack down on the rampant corruption allowed to fester in so many public housing authorities. Patterns of bribery, favoritism in contracting, and embezzlement undermine confidence that public resources can remain public.

It is the continuing shame of San Francisco that the voices of residents of public housing were pushed to the margins. Whether acknowledged or not, these activists were ahead of their time—confronting the consequences of austerity, not in a faraway land, but in their own neighborhoods. As Bethola Harper observed, "We asked hard questions about HOPE VI and tried our best to unite our neighbors, and we were treated like criminals for it. But I'm proud of what we were able to do with hardly any resources."

## Chapter Two
## Slow Burn: San Francisco's Hotel Residents Walk
## through the Fire

**February 24, 1999.** Former residents of the Hartland Hotel gathered in front of San Francisco's City Hall. Twelve days earlier, a fire consumed their home at Larkin and Geary in the Tenderloin. Among Hartland's residents were transgendered immigrants, minimum-wage workers, retirees, once and future opera singers, government aid recipients, a déclassé former member of Students for a Democratic Society, and black refugees from urban renewal wars past. The Mission Agenda, a poor people's organization, had gathered the residents from the various shelters they arrived at after the fire. The residents, unlike city officials, were not prone to mistake a shelter bed for a room of one's own. It was time to make that point clear.

The Hartland was just one of six residential hotels that burned in two years. The Star, Delta, Jerry, Leland, and Thor hotels were left blackened. Among residential hotel tenants, this left an eerie sense that someone was out to get them, possibly the landlord in an arson-for-profit scheme. It was something more sinister than arson: business-as-usual neglect. Exposed electrical systems, hallways so cluttered with debris they became a firetrap, a glum bouquet of the conditions that the city's poorest faced. High rents to live in small boxes, senior citizens trapped in their own rooms due to broken elevators and drug traffic. Despite this and perhaps because of it, hotel residents typically built tight networks of mutual aid to help each other survive. Life in residential hotels in the 1990s was a textbook case of legally enabled corruption and precarity. Landlords were not required to allow more than four overnight guests a month, yet rules could be bent for a bribe. Owners would routinely evict residents after twenty-eight days, in order to avoid eviction protections that kicked in after thirty days of tenancy, known as the practice of "musical rooms."

In the *New Mission News*, journalist Victor Miller described the loss of housing and community caused by the fires:

Burned out of the Thor Hotel, Carl Jones and his wife of 15 years were given three-week vouchers for the Mission Hotel. Management tossed them and their belongings out as soon as the vouchers expired and before they could gain permanent tenancy. Carl gets around in a wheelchair that also carries the oxygen canister he needs to breathe. When he lived at the Thor his fellow tenants carried him up and down the elevator-less hotel's stairs everyday. Around the corner from the Thor Tenants Union press conference, the couple waited to be taken to one of the city's homeless shelters where they would be separated. "This is the first time we've ever had to go to a shelter," Jacqueline said. Despite the gloominess of the moment Carl kept his sense of what was important "I'm one of the lucky ones, I found a good woman. Who else could love me through all of this?" he said.[1]

As the group entered City Hall, passing through metal detectors, some looked around the seat of local government unsure if they belonged there. The ornate building had recently been reopened after a multimillion-dollar renovation project. Majestic columns and a gigantic stairway were a stark contrast to the homeless shelters many had slept in the night before. Weaving a trail up the stairway to San Francisco City Hall, the tenants were greeted by one of the hundreds of grey-suited functionaries—the lifers at the Hall. "We know why you're here, and the sheriff has been called," remarked the day's designated flak-catcher.

"We want to talk to the mayor; we're going to be homeless if the city doesn't do something," yelled David McGuire, a Hartland resident who had become a leader in response to the fire epidemic. The city's "strategy" to deal with displacement by fire was to offer each survivor a two-week housing voucher through the Red Cross. The tenant's strategy was simple: help each other locate permanent housing through word of mouth and relationships with sympathetic social service agencies. At the end of each two-week span, those who had managed to wiggle past the musical room practice would join with those on the brink of homelessness again.[2]

Angry accusations of deft deflections of responsibility volleyed through City Hall. *The mayor is out of town. You don't care about us.*

*You need to make an appointment with the chief of staff.* Suddenly, the functionary decided that he had had enough contact with the rabble for one day. Retreating back into the mayor's office, he slammed the door, only to be met with a chorus of pounding fists. Soon the doors to the office were blockaded by those the city had forgot. "I had a little place to stay, but the fire took that away from me. Even though the Red Cross put me up at another hotel, I wasn't able to stay there. After that I was homeless. I stayed on the street and under bridges. The little bit of stuff I did salvage from the fire was taken from me by the police," testified Shirley Harrison, a resident of the Delta Hotel.[3]

This had been the drill for weeks, and it was working for the most part. They would occupy the mayor's office or the Red Cross or visit a landlord and demand permanent housing or an extension of the voucher for another few weeks. Fire survivors of one building would often take it upon themselves to comfort, advise, and organize subsequent victims. The fires ignited a season of protest outside of most "models" of organizing. With the Agenda, the residents relied on mutual aid and direct action casework to prevent homelessness of almost every survivor of the fires. As demonstrated by the example of Carl's neighbors carrying his wheelchair up flights of stairs, many hotel residents are excellent at forming survival networks. These networks between people are designed to help each other live through trying circumstances by providing the things that the state and economy can't—or won't—provide. In a typical hotel, this can mean watching a neighbor during drug use to avoid overdose, wellness checks for elders and the infirm, or the sharing of HIV meds.

Another torched hotel, the Thor, was an example of how, in many cases, self-organizing and strategic community organizing can complement each other. The hotel was typical of many in the 1990s— charging exorbitant rents, restricting visitors to four overnight visits a month, and circumventing the rent ordinance by tossing tenants to the streets before legal protections could kick in. (San Francisco Rent Ordinance grants tenants rights after twenty-eight.) Remarked Thor Hotel resident leader, Bobbie Inglis, "What the city has to realize is we didn't just lose rooms in a hotel, we lost our homes, our community. That's what we're trying to replace here. Hotels profit, tenants lose, the city loses. What we had here was people, whether on GA or

SSI or Workfare, who managed their affairs in peace. Isn't it worth it to replace something like that?"[4]

At the Thor Hotel, many of the worst conditions had begun to change. With the Agenda doing much of the groundwork, the Mission SRO Collaborative had helped the tenants to form a tenants association and press the City Attorney's office to enforce codes and crack down on illegal evictions.[5] At the time of the fire, many residents had achieved permanent status and became strong voices for tenant rights in the larger movement.

### Building an Agenda

The corner of 16th and Mission streets in San Francisco is a living room for people who don't have living rooms. The Mission Agenda built its membership there by hosting regular Hotel Hollers, reminiscent of the sidewalk soapboxing of turn-of-the-century activists. The formula was simple: bring a bullhorn, invite people to speak up about conditions in their hotels, police brutality, or just about anything on their minds. Then identify people with actionable grievances or the type of analysis that might make them a valuable asset in organizing.

Political speeches are rarely as blunt as those found at the Hollers. "What we have now is the *four-fuck* rule. Ask anyone living in any other kind of housing if they would ever live in a place where the landlord says you can have only four visitors a month. If you live in a residential hotel you have to ration your overnight stays, and you are unlucky, if you get lucky, after you have used yours up," explained Mike Dorn, a resident at the Mission Hotel. The Hollers also showcased an incredible amount of musical talent. Usually, Dorn's street corner speeches would be followed by an a cappella version of Billie Holiday's "I Gotta Right to Sing the Blues," provided by Daphne "Chocolate" Benson, or an original song from Carlos Guitarlos, a white-bearded bluesman transplanted from Los Angeles to the corner of 16th and Valencia. Hotel Hollers weren't just a point of political recruitment, but a celebration of local people's culture, community, and dreams deferred but never fully forgotten.

The concept of direct action casework guided many of the Agenda's most successful efforts, such as the response to the fire epidemic. This version of casework combines legal advocacy with political direct action. For example, if a resident were to come into the Agenda's offices looking for help with an eviction, the organization's volunteers would help her connect with the appropriate social service organizations and help decode the volumes of paperwork needed to file a response. If and when legal and administrative channels proved unhelpful, the Agenda would plan public actions to directly pressure the landlord.[6]

The Agenda was founded by two roommates: Richard Marquez and Chris Daly, neither residential hotel residents. Marquez was a native San Franciscan, long-time organizer, and professional social worker, who had been involved with immigrant rights organizing for many years, with a small organization called AYUDA ("help" in Spanish). AYUDA began as a self-help organization for homeless Latinos. In the mid-1990s, organized groups of white supremacists started videotaping and intimidating day laborers looking for work in the Mission. AYUDA shifted gears and began confronting the racists with counter-protests. Marquez had a magnetic charisma, and relished direct door-to-door outreach, even if it meant sneaking onto a fire escape or pushing the boundaries of his city-issued social work-er's identification to convince hotel operators to let him past the front desk. Daly arrived in San Francisco in 1993 to work with Empty the Shelters, a student organization dedicated to working in solidarity with anti-poverty organizations. The duo began organizing around the corner at the Mission Hotel, where they met Dorn and a recent parolee from state prison, Danny McClendon.

Their office, a block away from the BART (Bay Area Rapid Transit) station, became a social center for local hotel residents, including former Black Panther Al Thompson, well-known sex worker activist Duran Ruiz, and neighborhood staples such as Vietnam veteran Kennard Jones, retired unionist Tony Hester, and consummate volunteer office worker Beverly Bramlett.

The Agenda viewed itself as champion of the other San Francisco, those completely jettisoned by the blooming dot-com economy and often marginalized in social justice discourse. Hotel Hollers gradually morphed into nighttime anti-gentrification pub crawls where residents would set up shop in front of gentrifying bars and nightspots, shaming patrons and speaking out about an increasingly unrecognizable neighborhood. The Agenda received a lot criticism from those who viewed the actions as pointless, target-less, and un-strategic. For Agenda members, these actions were an important part of speaking back to those who they perceived held the power, even if this section of the gentry had little to do with the complex web of real estate developers, politicians, and landlords who controlled the political economy of the Mission District.

The Mission Agenda's style and approach were similar to two important movements: the unemployed workers' movements of the Great Depression and the post–civil rights movement welfare rights organizing. During the 1930s, radical activists formed unemployed councils, concerned with fighting for a basic survival program against hunger and poverty. When a neighbor was denied relief, organizers would often shut down relief offices. During this time, less than thirty years before the dawn of the civil rights movement, the movement blazed a trail by incorporating a racial analysis into its defense of working-class people as a whole. The councils rallied against discrimination in the rehiring of unemployed workers, not only because of race but gender and religion as well.

The most dramatic tactic was the anti-eviction struggle led by the councils—a movement that was strongest in New York and Detroit. Using a block committee structure, the councils effectively mobilized against evictions. This structure allowed a simple and succinct response to evictions. Neighbors, often numbering in the thousands, would physically intervene in evictions.

The unemployed councils reached a national fervor, with mass demonstrations in New York, Detroit, Chicago, Seattle, and San Francisco. In some cities, the demonstrations were incredibly sedate, such as in San Francisco, where they were attended by the City council and chief of police. In other areas, more militant tactics collided with local authorities. The scope of the movement, which had links with organized labor through the CIO, presented a threat to the established order of relief. Actions like these served a double purpose: they provided relief and at the same time called into question the legitimacy of capitalism. The intense pressure of the unemployed council movement led to key demands became incorporated into New Deal programs and other wartime economic interventions, even leading to national wartime rent controls.[7]

Had the Agenda been born a few decades earlier, they would have fit into the National Welfare Rights Organization's (NWRO) model of mobilizing people around government assistance. The NWRO's ultimate goal was to establish a guaranteed adequate income for all Americans, and they took action around their member's immediate needs such as increased monthly benefits, the end of stringent eligibility requirements, and invasive methods used by social workers.

In their summation of the NWRO's work, Frances Fox Piven and Richard Cloward asserted that the poor people's organizations should primarily mobilize disruptive protest instead of building new leaders attached to the group.[8] The Agenda's fire campaigns proved part of their point: disruptive protest can sometimes be the *only* thing that cuts through the morass of social service bureaucracy and government indifference. Indeed, a flexible definition of membership had to be eventually adopted in response to the multiple pressures Agenda regulars faced in their everyday lives. Yet the Agenda provided a space where residential hotel tenants could and did learn the ropes of organizing and play important decision-making roles in the organization.

In order to understand residential hotels (also know as Single room occupancy, or SROs) it is important to grasp one important fact: they are homes. For some, they are homes of last resort, for others they are comfortable, tiny dwellings—long before urban planners and developers began promoting "micro units" as a solution to the housing crisis. "Residential Hotels are the least expensive and most easily accessed housing for people who might have trouble finding other housing," said long-time residential hotel resident and former Mission Agenda activist Susan Marsh.

Typically, the rooms are small, dozens to a floor, and the bathrooms and kitchens are shared in common. In the years after the 1906 earthquake, they were built quickly, all over the city. They were inhabited, up until the 1960s, by Sailors Union of the Pacific men; International Longshore and Warehouse Union retirees, who appreciated the flexible nature of the tenancy; white, black, and filipino senior citizens; and even a few middle-class residents. While some were dilapidated, many weren't.

## Residential Hotels as Canaries in the Housing Coal Mine

Residential hotels are depicted over and over again in literature. For Charles Bukowski and Jack Kerouac, they were "flophouses," seedy and fertile ground for their stories and poems; many of San Francisco's hotels are visited in Hammett's *The Maltese Falcon*. Political currents also run through. Valerie Solanas, who attempted to assassinate Andy Warhol, died in the Tenderloin's Bristol Hotel in 1988. In 1973, the last of the American Indian Movement's Alcatraz Island occupiers were taken to the Senator Hotel, where arresting federal marshals paid for a single night's stay for the crew, who held their closing rituals and final press conference in the lobby.

The fire epidemic of the 1990s was not the first time that residential hotel tenants had taken it on the chin. About 4,500 units of residential hotels were demolished in the 1960s and 1970s as part of San Francisco's urban renewal push. In their place went luxury hotels, museums, condominiums, and other businesses. The intent was to create a higher tax base, seen as necessary to the future of the city in the face of de-industrialization. San Francisco's port, the site of pivotal working-class movements such as the 1934 General Strike, was on its last-legs due to mechanization and a strategic choice by the shipping industry to concentrate operations in Oakland.[9] The formula was nearly identical to the process in the Western Addition: declare a neighborhood "blighted" despite any evidence to the contrary, make meager buyout offers to owners, seize property, and hand it over to private developers. Today, where residential hotels once flourished on Howard Street is a fountain monument to Dr. Martin Luther King Jr., looking out onto the Moscone Convention Center, a Target Store, and millionaires' condominiums.

On August 4th, 1977, thousands of people blockaded the eviction of the International Hotel (I-Hotel) in San Francisco's Manilatown. The blockade signified the end of a decade-long campaign to save the hotel and the mostly elderly Filipino retirees from eviction. Reflecting the politics of the era, the I-Hotel defense was seen by many as an opportunity to exercise anti-imperialist ideals on the local level. Many of the *manongs* (elders) had fled repression in the Philippines, were World War II veterans, and had labored in California's Central Valley farms. Local real estate magnate Walter Shorenstein sold the building to the Four Seas Development Corporation, located in Hong Kong. The decade-long campaign became a touchstone for the emerging Asian-American left, but also drew in local churches, trade unions, community groups, and revolutionary organizations. While the sheriff evicted the seniors through brute force, the alliances formed on the front lines were pivotal in the growing affordable housing movement and in passing, two years later, of rent control.[10] The fact that Manilatown was permanently wiped off of San Francisco's map by redevelopment sets it apart from similar struggles in the Western Addition and South of Market, which at least retained a portion of their original communities. It wouldn't be the last time that the fate of a residential hotel would come to symbolize a much more acute virus in the urban housing system.

### New Rules for Traumatized Radicals

The Mission Agenda's main accomplishments were the response to the fire epidemic and the enfranchisement of those often left out of social change conversations. The Hotel Hollers were brilliant in their simplicity, making the rhetoric of "giving voice-to-the-voiceless" real by simply handing them the bullhorn. It touched on spatial politics by claiming for poor people an area contested by police crackdowns and gentrification. As we will see in Chapter 4, co-founder of the Mission Agenda Chris Daly became a city supervisor in 2000, part of a progressive-populist electoral sweep. The Mission Agenda closed in 2003, and with it San Francisco lost an important player in the fight for an open, inclusive city.

The Agenda's impact could have been greater if organizers had fully strategized around the complexities of organizing people who are largely traumatized by poverty. Much of the left has always been conflicted about the role of poor people, perhaps because few of us have experienced the extreme poverty faced every day by the Agenda's stalwarts. The left's poverty binary often destroys its best intentions. Some sections marginalize poor people through flagrant abuse of Marx's writing on the lumpen proletariat—certain groups of people are permanently unorganizable and prone to criminal activity. Eerily, this mirrors the right's conflation of long-term poverty with criminality. Yet others (and this was the case with the Agenda) fetishized poor people as the only source of revolutionary change, the only ones with the interest and real insight to get the job done. Both poles are like empty vases waiting to be filled with the class and race anxieties of those who claim to have the interest of poor people at heart. The very real potential for impoverished people to lead and determine their own destiny is replaced with radical others' fantasies about them or rationales for ignoring their voices.

In the Agenda's case, it also led to ignoring the role of trauma in the lives of the people being organized. Living in slum conditions, and facing the aggregate impacts of poverty leaves its own scars. By the time the Agenda folded, many of its shining stars were dead— some of overdoses, others of untreated health conditions; others dropped out of movement work entirely, citing burnout. This is not to accuse the Agenda of murder. The fact was that organizing with the Agenda could be grueling. The expectations put on volunteers rivaled those put on trade union staff or a vanguard organization. The unclear lines of leadership often left decisions to those with the most passionate denunciation of oppression. Yet a lack of common analysis of what oppression actually meant to the organization reduced disagreements to constantly fluctuating individualistic definitions. This led to long arguments that became more and more personal as time went on.

In order to deal with the very real personal tolls that life under racialized capitalism extracts, organizing must become informed by the experiences of trauma. This does not mean replacing collective action with an endless series of encounter sessions and self-care substituting itself for societal change. In fact, there were several incidents in the 1960s and '70s where the incursion of psychotherapy into radical organizing bolstered the hands of manipulative demagogues.[11] Organizers should at least be competent in the basics of trauma recovery.

Joe Wilson, a lifelong community organizer, has dedicated much of his work to bridging the gap between healing trauma and challenging the system. He directs the Healing, Organizing & Leadership Development (HOLD) program at San Francisco's Hospitality House. He defines trauma as the "impairment of the body's natural physical and emotional capacity to heal itself."

Collective trauma by extension is the destruction of a community's ability to find solutions to the problems it faces due to the aggregated injuries of inequality and discrimination. Wilson grew up on Chicago's South Side and describes himself as "being radicalized by the Mayor Daley regime."

Wilson advocates "gently, but consistently pushing individuals to connect with others in some way, no matter how small, so that healing is seen as part of reconnection, renewal, and taking more active part in community life, and community empowerment."[12]

For example, a core principle in recovery is the empowerment of survivors. Almost all community organizations claim to empower the people in their base communities. While the process of gaining skills and confidence to act can be healing, it must be met with a commitment to a transparent use of power and an ethical stewardship of people's stories. Just as consent is central to a healing relationship, so is it toward building welcoming, strong organizations. In therapy, a key tenet of recovery is restoring individual autonomy. Healthy organizations can model this by building collective self-determination and power over the larger conditions that wreak havoc in people's lives. Alinsky's model defacto signed off on using whatever it takes to mobilize people toward the greater good—letting the means always justify the ends. Some forms of left organizing, though posing as Alinsky's antidote, replicate this grindhouse approach to social change through reliance on rigid hierarchies and corrosive dynamics between "organizers" (paid staff) and "leaders" (volunteers from the community). It is impossible for larger societal dynamics to be completely barricaded from the work of social change. However, the relationship between organizers and the organized should not mirror that of colonizer and the colonized.

Recovery from trauma has three phases: the establishment of safety, remembrance and mourning, and reconnection with ordinary life. The best organizing, particularly with those under the boot of oppression, adds another step: the ability to imagine what a better future might look like, for one's self and community. As Allison Lum, a former SRO resident and fire survivor, recalled, "While some may think that living under oppressive hotel conditions makes for complacency and puts people to sleep, the anger of injustice combined with the proximity of mutual need on the most basic level, proves to be a breeding ground for tapping into class consciousness and organizing for positive change."

# Chapter Three
## They Plan for Profits, We Plan for People: Local Politics and International Conversations in the Mission District

**September 27, 2013.** On this day, renowned Mission District artist Guillermo Gómez-Peña wrote an open letter to his colleague, René Yañez. After three decades of residency in the neighborhood, Yañez and his wife were being evicted.

It seems that we no longer have a citizenry but rather a virtual mob. I see them everyday, the hordes of iPad and iPhone texting zombies, oblivious to us and our lives, our inspirations and our tribulations. I see them in my building and on the street, invading the city with an attitude of unchecked entitlement, taking over every square inch and squeezing out the last drops of otherness. I see them outside of my studio on 24th and Bryant wondering "How much does the weird native guy pay for rent?"; getting ready to make their outrageous bid to our landlord. 300% increase?

No problem. City Hall has their back!

Our city has became a bohemian theme park for consumer fools with the latest gadgets in hand, but what happens when there are no more bohemians left? In the meantime we are all sadly witnessing, day by day, how funky, decades-old Mexican restaurants and immigrants bars full of memories and ghosts get replaced overnight by upscale eateries and theme bars for twenty-somethings; the old billiard halls, specialty stores, beauty parlors, and *carnicerias* become "smart cafes" and "gourmet bakeries" for a new clientele who might as well live in Dallas or San Diego. Thousands of artists have moved to Oakland or further away, sometimes back to their hometowns. I myself have lost at least 30 performance art colleagues in the last 5 years. I cannot stand the thought of losing you as well.

Gómez-Peña's letter unpeeled the multiple ways that people experience a neighborhood in the spasms of displacement. As homes are lost, so too are the things that make cities valuable: sanctuary, memory, culture, and community. Yañez's impending eviction represented the destruction of all four. He was responsible for bringing the Dia de los Muertos celebration to the Mission, founding the Galería de la Raza and other Latino cultural institutions, while mentoring a generation of radical artists.[1]

"In my block, what I see is people getting evicted, at the same time as a great deal of cultural tourism. There is going to be just enough left of Latino culture to provide the illusion of Latinism or Chingonismo," remarked Yañez.[2]

In 2013 the housing movement was reinvigorated and took to the streets once more. With evictions quickly cannibalizing the remains of the city's housing stock, the city's tech industry loomed large in activist crosshairs. Resurgent tech, whose bubble was thought to be burst in 2000 was back with a vengeance, with 1,700 firms employing 44,000 people.[3] The vast majority of those people migrated from places far afield. Simple laws of competition pitted tech workers, whose median starting wage is $123,000, against the rest of the city for housing already in scarce supply.[4] According to the Anti-Eviction Mapping Project, a volunteer effort that researches the impacts and causes of displacement, evictions were up 115 percent in 2013 over the previous year.[5]

The clear-cutting of San Francisco's affordable housing has resulted in an atmosphere that can best be described as "Tech versus Everyone Else." In September of 2013, activists associated with Eviction Free San Francisco began blockading the now-infamous "Google Buses," private corporate buses that transport techies from their neighborhoods in San Francisco to the corporate headquarters of Google, Facebook, MTV, and others in nearby Silicon Valley. The tactic was simple: surround the bus and don't let anyone get to work on time. The series of protests drew international media attention to San Francisco's displacement epidemic. But the meaning of protests was contested, even by the protesters themselves: some insisted that they wanted the techies to join the movement against displacement, viewing them as simply high-paid pawns in the game. And others made little distinction between a Facebook employee and Mark Zuckerberg, the company's boy-wonder founder whose personal net worth hovers around $27 billion—roughly equivalent to the Gross Domestic Product of Bolivia.[6] It was a fascinating case of *indirect* action. The blockades put a face on displacement even if it would be impossible to know who on the bus, if anyone, had actually displaced someone. The actions tapped the politics of resentment. Who were these people who expected their own private transportation system when the rest of us had to take the city bus? Why were the buses allowed to park in public bus stops? A parent doing the same thing, dropping their kid off at an appointment, for example, would risk a $271 ticket.

Yañez's eviction illustrates the mechanics of how property speculation works to displace long-term residents. Golden Properties Limited Liability Company (LLC) purchased the four-unit building he lived in. While represented by a single individual, Sergio Iantorno, the LLC typically gathers several investors in a legal entity, which shields their other investments from legal action and can be used to obscure ownership. Used in the private market, it is a tool to minimize oversight while maximizing profits.

Yañez and his family paid $450 a month for rent, though rents in the same neighborhood now start at $2,700. This is a monumental "rent gap" (the difference between what a property is earning for an owner and what it *could* earn). In most housing markets, buildings with multiple apartments in them fetch a much higher price if sold separately as tenancy-in-common schemes rather than as a single building. Say that Yañez's landlord bought the whole building for $1.5 million dollars and went on to sell each unit for $750,000 to individual investors.

The Mission District's plight, and that of the larger city, is reminiscent of another tech boom, in the 1990s. (Ironically, Yañez fought off an eviction then as well.) The previous boom died an unceremonious death and took with it a host of firms whose names are scarcely remembered today. However, the unresolved issues from the final decade of the twentieth century cast a long shadow today. How can housing affordable to lower- and middle-income people be preserved in a market economy? What types of goals should urban social movements adopt to prevent displacement? How can concerns of representation and authenticity in a city pockmarked by race and class inequalities be addressed?

## The Past as Prophecy

*"No more gold domes, we want real homes!"* chanted tenant activist Tommi Avicolli-Mecca, as a long line of people approached San Francisco City Hall. The opulent renovations, one of Mayor Willie Brown's legacy projects, had become a symbol of the anxieties of a city feeling the spasms of displacement. Brown, the city's first black mayor, was a masterful politician who had served over three decades in the State Assembly. Four years before, he was elected in a landslide victory against Mayor Frank Jordan, a former police officer and final standard-bearer for San Francisco's old-school white leadership.

The Brown era was shaping up to be a study in contradictions. The city was in the midst of a boom time hailed by many as a second Gold Rush. Silicon Valley was moving north from the Peninsula. On a weekly basis, new dot-com startups opened, gobbling up all available office and industrial spaces. This new economy was changing the character of San Francisco, with residential rents doubling citywide, but especially in the working-class Mission District. The Mission, with its ornate Victorian houses, ample cultural amenities, warm (for San Francisco) weather, and proximity to downtown was particularly appealing to property speculators.

What was happening was much bigger than Brown. Speculative capital, let off the chain from decades of disinvestment and free trade, had finally found a home in the neighborhood. Venture capitalists, once marked by their fiscal restraint, seemed to be handing out cash to new companies with no discernable products or even business plans. As early as 1992, the Mission District showed signs of a massive displacement push. Well-heeled workers from around the globe came to take part in the frenzy. Residential evictions of long-time residents skyrocketed, and long-time Latino cultural institutions were displaced altogether.

Even as the city's character shifted again, Brown looked around and declared that nothing was wrong. In Brown's world, gentrification's antagonists were gentrifiers themselves, while real working-class people had voluntarily moved on to better housing in the suburbs. Brown had gone to bat to make sure that there were plenty of pans in the stream during the new Gold Rush. The master of the deal, he convinced his friends in Sacramento to find comfortable bureaucratic jobs for members of the Board of Supervisors, allowing him to appoint loyalists. The Brown board made sure that his political backers were taken care off; developers were given minimal scrutiny, attacks on rent control encouraged, and those who dared question the city's trajectory marginalized.

The March of the Evicted (named in reference to the European March of the Excluded)had hiked a mile and a half from 16th and Mission Streets.[7] Organizers had expected about two hundred attendees, but over five times that many showed up. In planning meetings, they had decided to keep the march on the sidewalk and applied for permits, to protect immigrants and people with entanglements with the law. Those very same people led the march into the streets, police be damned. The march, held two days before Halloween in 1999, indicated that the outrage against displacement might turn into something big.

Consider the depths of a decade of displacement: nearly 17,500 formal, "no-fault" evictions filed with the Rent Arbitration and Stabilization Board between 1990 and 2000. Ted Gullicksen of the San Francisco Tenants Union estimates that this number could be doubled if all those who moved at the mere threat of eviction are considered.[8] It was not until the final years of the decade that the disparate strands of the fight started to coalesce into a coherent urban movement. The most visible actor in this moment was the Mission Anti-Displacement Coalition (MAC), which utilized a sophisticated mix of direct action, lobbying, and electoral mobilization while modeling what popular power could eventually look like.[9]

### The Gathering Storm

In 1999, the media latched on to the case of eighty-two-year-old Lola McKay who became a symbol of the eviction madness and helped to galvanize political opposition to displacement. McKay's home of forty years was bought by the John Hickey Brokerage. Hoping to sell each of the four units in the building separately, the firm moved to evict her. Homes delivered vacant to new buyers are more valuable than occupied ones, as prospective buyers often balk at the cost and the ethics of evicting tenants. With virtually no support network or family, McKay vowed to fight to the end for the right to live in her home. A collection of groups including the San Francisco Tenants Union and the Senior Housing Action Collaborative began a campaign with a single demand: a lifetime lease for McKay. Although it would have been easy to grant this and still make an enormous profit on the three vacant units, the brokerage did not relent. Activists occupied the offices of their lawyers, Wiegel & Fried. Television coverage shifted between McKay and a protest that resulted in a broken window and an altercation with a security guard.

The action changed the displacement narrative in the mainstream media; gone temporarily was the story of sympathetic first-time homeowners fulfilling the American Dream. This episode exposed an eviction industry that wouldn't think twice about evicting your grandmother. McKay died not long after her eviction, but her fight helped to bring anti-displacement politics into the mainstream. "Lola McKay's case stood for seniors who have to fight for their rights in this city, and unfortunately Lola died for these rights. Her case ripped the mask off of the evictors and revealed them to be property speculators, not just small property owners trying to exercise their property rights," explained Barbara Blong of the Senior Action Network.

The McKay actions were simply the most visible of many spirited protests and "landlord visits" by tenant activists in the 1990s. Other actions shut down landlords' places of business, such as when the owner of a flower shop attempted to evict a person in the latter stages of AIDS. At one protest a ninety-two-year-old woman who had spent time in the French Resistance against Nazi occupation declared, "I have shot fascists dead in the streets of Europe, so I will not let a petty landlord drive me from my home."

The eviction crisis was intensified by a landlord assault on the ability of cities in California to enact meaningful rent control. San Francisco's Rent Arbitration and Stabilization Ordinance was passed in 1979. The ordinance outlined thirteen just causes for eviction, limited rent increases and created a regulatory agency to mediate in landlord-tenant disputes. In 1986, the California State Legislature passed the Ellis Act that allowed landlords to clear a building of tenants if they intended to remove the building from the rental market altogether. Landlords argued that Ellis simply allowed property owners to change uses of their property, yet the real estate industry was quick to exploit the opening for property speculation.

San Francisco's rent control ordinance has always lacked vacancy control, meaning that landlords could raise the rent to whatever the market could bear between tenancies. This created a situation where long-term tenants, particularly seniors and families, were targeted for eviction. In 1996, the landlord lobby passed the Costa-Hawkins Act, which got rid of vacancy control and made single-family homes ineligible for rent control protections. Emboldened by victories on the state level, landlords placed Proposition E, which would eliminate protections on smaller buildings, on San Francisco's ballot, but a "No on E" campaign defeated the measure by two-thirds of the vote. It was the partial deregulation of private housing stock that left seniors like McKay vulnerable.

The depth of anger against displacement was also reflected in the case of the Mission Yuppie Eradication Project (MYEP), an insurrectional poster campaign. Its first campaign urged people to trash yuppie cars, the second implored readers to attack and destroy upscale bars "in the next major urban riot," and a third predicted that the luxury lofts popping up would become "future squats of America."

A long-time fixture in the local activist scene, Kevin Keating became the face of MYEP. The San Francisco Police Department arrested Keating for making terrorist threats, and his collection of Situationist and Marxist books were seized and served a much longer time in detention than he did. This thrust Keating, a white East Coast transplant, into the media spotlight, making him the recognized voice of anti-gentrification on the national stage. Using the *nom de guerre* Nestor Makhno (after the Ukrainian anarchist),[10] he appeared on the *Bill Maher Show* and was interviewed (and often treated to lunch by reporters at the types of restaurants he decried) for the *New York Times* and ABC News.

The posters did not catalyze the massive resistance Keating had hoped for. One drunken progressive lawyer did in fact attempt to vandalize a sport utility vehicle outside of a Mexican restaurant on Valencia Street. The vehicle belonged to the restaurant's immigrant dishwashers, who owned it collectively. One live-work loft under construction was damaged by arson and quickly repaired thanks to insurance. The *SF Weekly* newspaper capitalized on the media circus by publishing a fake ad for a "Stop the Hate" rally and had a field day of snark when angry counter protesters showed up at Dolores Park to make a stand against the prank.

MYEP wasn't a complete failure. It was one of the few anti-gentrification projects (at the time) to openly talk about capitalism's role in out-of-control development. In Keating's words, "I started by targeting the material possessions of the bourgeois invaders; their cars, the entertainment spots that drew them to the Mission District, then their luxury housing complexes. Given the mass psychology of contemporary consumer society this was exactly the right place to begin; waving the red flag of property destruction put the ball in play quickly and dramatically. As the posters became notorious I should have supplemented the poster campaign with a strategy for further action. I didn't do this."[11]

The campaign highlighted the sharp limits of electoral engage-ment, even if the alternative of constant illegal activity found only a small audience. MYEP also projected alienation, too common to ultra-left projects and their spokespeople, which was reflected in an inability to engage with everyday people and other activists who weren't radical enough. The revolution, it ended up, was not just a poster campaign away.

## The Call Was for Unity

In other corners of the neighborhood, the call was for unity, broad coalition, and experimentation with multiple tactics. People Orga-nized to Demand Environmental and Economic Rights (PODER), the Mission Agenda, St. Peter's Housing Committee, the Day Labor program, and Mission Housing Development Corporation founded the Mission Anti-Displacement Coalition (MAC). Each organi-zation had done respectable work separately—defending the rights of residential hotel tenants, fighting immigrant discrimination and evictions, or building low-income housing. MAC represented a more coordinated, broader attempt to work together toward a different vision of the city. MAC recognized that the fight was on multiple fronts, combining Direct Action with electoral mobilization. MAC could also turn out hundreds of people for planning commission meetings. Internally, the coalition defined gentrification as the local expression of global neoliberal economics and a continuance of domestic colonial practice.[12]

MAC grew in the wake of a corporate takeover of the gentrification process. After Mayor Brown's Board of Supervisors approved the 160,000 square foot Bryant Square project—a gigantic dot-com office development in the middle of the Mission—residents mobilized in unprecedented numbers. The plan was to demolish an entire city block on Bryant Street, displacing several community-serving businesses and low-income artist studios. The project sponsor, Southern California-based Stein Kingsley Stein Corporation (SKS), pushed for approval even though it was acknowledged that planting this sort of development in the middle of a residential neighborhood would fuel evictions. SKS had plenty of money to buy friends, including artist and Latino social service agencies, and some arts organizations did accept offers of bargain space. MAC, bolstered by a report by Joint Venture Silicon Valley, pointed out that most of the jobs would not go to local residents and that any promises of community benefits could not outweigh the damage.[13]

Previously, most of San Francisco's housing activism had centered around expanding rent control, building more affordable housing, or defending a specific building against eviction. MAC opened up a new front by targeting the city's planning process. They brought the network of Planning Department staff, permit expediters, developers, and mayoral appointees to the department's commission into public view. With little consideration of the social impacts, the Planning Department fast-tracked the approvals of high-end development projects in many cases, completely ignoring regulations like the replacement of demolished units and community review of controversial projects.

In past decades, the threat of displacement came directly from the government through urban renewal projects, while developers waited in the wings to take advantage of the decimation. In the 1990s, developers were in the vanguard, buying and speculating on property. State intervention was more covert, with arcane zoning codes routinely drafted to facilitate maximum profits while those designed to protect neighborhoods were ignored. "City government still aided and abetted displacement. They allowed loopholes in the live-work ordinance, and refused to protect long-term residents," explained Antonio Diaz, an organizer with PODER.[14]

The decision to challenge the way the city was planned had both practical and existential implications. The Planning Department was the locus of development in San Francisco, and its commission made the decisions that could make or break working-class neighborhoods. The Planning Commission rarely examined the displacement potential of high-end projects. On a broader level, MAC also challenged the notion of rational city planning and highlighted the real class and racial implications of the process. They pointed to the potential of transformative planning where popular participation was not reduced to the process of toothless predetermined community meetings. MAC saw the neighborhood as the "geographical space and the material basis of the cultures that inhabited it."[15]

A May 28, 2000 community "accountability session" at Horace Mann Elementary School, with Planning Department director Gerald Green and Planning Commission president Hector Chinchilla in attendance, gathered over five hundred angry attendees.[16] Local residents such as Olga Cardona testified about the trauma of seeing friends and family removed.[17] "We're here today to express our outrage—outrage over the displacement of our community due to the rapid invasion of dot-com office complexes and luxury lofts," proclaimed long-time Mission activist Santiago Ruiz. He pointed out that a new luxury development with a $500,000 price tag per unit was far out of step with a neighborhood where the median income was about $30,000. At that meeting, 850,000 square feet of tech office space was approved by the Planning Department for the Mission District—the equivalent of two Transamerica Pyramid towers.[18]

Neither Green nor Chinchilla agreed to any of MAC's core demands, which were:

- An immediate moratorium on new market-rate housing and live-work lofts in the Mission.
- An immediate moratorium on office conversions and new construction of dot-com office space in the Mission.
- An immediate end to all illegal conversions.
- A community planning process to rezone the Mission District.

While the city's planning regime had the power to alter the face of the Mission, Chinchilla denied that it had the power to protect residents: "You have to understand that the Planning Department has no authority to impose a moratorium."

In preparing for a July 13 march to the Planning Department's offices, MAC activists vigorously debated whether or not to use direct action to shut it down. One group was concerned that premature militancy would alienate the growing numbers of working-class Latino families drawn to the coalition's work. The other felt that without disruptive tactics, city government would have little incentive to listen to their demands. After a narrow vote, an occupation was nixed. However, as the march neared the offices, the department shut itself down to friends and foes alike.[19] The Planning Commission routinely barred MAC activists from entering their meetings and at one point City Hall sheriffs forced a non-violent activist, Jonathan Youtt, to the ground.

At the intersection of Mission and 14th streets lies the gigantic former National Guard Armory. Built in 1912, the castle-like building has always played a dubious role in San Francisco's class politics, having served as a command center for suppressing the 1934 General Strike. Closed in 1976, the site remained vacant as few could imagine what to do with such a massive building, protected as a historic landmark. Finally, in 2000, Eikon Investments purchased it and announced that it would redevelop the site as a gigantic office space for arriving tech firms. At the grand opening, celebrants, arriving in luxury cars, were greeted by Latino activists who demanded a different path for the building: a school, affordable housing, a health clinic.[20] Oscar Grande, a life-long San Franciscan and an organizer with PODER, says they were drawing a line in gentrification's sand. "We knew they did not have the power to stop the Armory from becoming office space for tech. We knew we could use it to begin to tell our side of the story. How the industry and their choices were impacting the lives and livelihoods of our community. We went out here with neighborhood youth—two particular young people, Olga Cardona and Lily Gonzales, went into the start up grand opening/party and started chanting in the space, they got on the mic talking shit to the party goers."

On September 21, 2000, fifteen people were arrested for occupying the offices of Bigstep.com, a company that displaced dozens of community-service agencies when it moved into the Bayview Building, a bleak looking piece of modernist architecture at 21st and Mission streets. The start-up's CEO, who assured them that he was a progressive and had protested South African apartheid during college, greeted occupiers. Outside, a community dialogue on displacement was ignited as MAC activists scaled the building and hung a banner reading "Profit Takes a Bigstep on the Heart of Community," while beneath, bilingual agitators passed out flyers for the next MAC meeting.[21]

"Taking direct action at Bigstep.com was important in MAC's development. It was a moment of radicalization, with many community members doing a nonviolent civil disobedience for the first time in their lives. It was also an experiment in inclusiveness and creativity. We combined the civil disobedience inside with outreach and a rally outside, where people on probation, parole, or with immigration status or family concerns led outreach on the street, and spoke out about displacement. It gave us a sense of our power, and of the effectiveness of leveraging a range of tactics," remarked Maria Poblet, an organizer with Saint Peter's Housing Committee.[22]

On numerous other occasions, Planning Commission meetings were stacked, and many times shut down altogether. A *caminata* (procession) throughout the neighborhood attracted over five thousand people. While the Lola McKay actions had helped to put a human face on the displaced, MAC, as a multiracial movement willing to work both within and outside the legislative system, took the debate a step further. They became skilled advocates and researchers on alternative planning processes, yet also shut down the Planning Department multiple times.[23]

Fernando Marti, active in MAC at the time, recalls the complexities of incorporating direct -action tactics into the coalition's repertoire: "One difficult aspect of direct action was how our Latino base could be involved, especially the undocumented or families with multiple jobs. We depended on a smaller cadre, who was willing to take risk of arrest. But a critique I think is that the direct actions were primarily symbolic, meant to get press attention and change the public dialogue, and not the kind of incremental direct actions where the people could see themselves taking greater power *for themselves.*"

## Histories of Resistance

The Spanish conquest began in 1776. Like today's exiled, the surviving Ohlone Indians fled across the bay to what is now Oakland and Hayward. An Indian uprising failed, and the tribe's population was reduced from about 1.5 million people to less than two thousand.[24] By 1841, there were only fifty Ohlone left in the area that would become known as the Mission. In addition to the genocide, the Spanish also brought with them another European innovation: the practice of private property and parceling out lands once held in common.

The first gold rush, in 1848, helped develop San Francisco, and the Mission in particular. Most of the prospectors looking for gold found little or none, but the industries created to serve them, like Levi's Jeans (located at 14th and Valencia) became new empires. Even in its early days, the Mission's working class had a sizable Latino flavor. At the turn of the century, trade with Latin America brought coffee giants such as Hills Brothers to the city, while upheaval associated with the construction of the Panama Canal and the Mexican Revolution brought new immigrants to the Mission. The neighborhood became a hotbed of radical working-class activity. The anarchist Emma Goldman briefly lived on Dolores Street. Industries rapidly unionized. The Labor Temple at 16th and Mission became one of the union command centers for the 1934 General Strike. The Mission was distinctly a working person's neighborhood and an immigrant one of Latino, Irish, and Italian hues.[25]

The Mission District's history of community organizing informed and ultimately confronted MAC. In 1966, San Francisco Redevelopment Agency had its eye on the Mission District, to prepare the neighborhood for the arrival of the Bay Area Rapid Transit (BART) system. As urban renewal plans often do, they united conservative populists (resenting big government interference in private property) with the radical left (who saw the plan as an example of domestic colonial mindset.) Between these polls were churches, worker organizations, service organizations, and welfare rights groups. A Redevelopment Agency drawing of the reinvented neighborhood showed shiny glass buildings and transit plazas, but little trace of the existing neighborhoods remained. The obvious question for long-time residents (as it is today) was "Where am I in this picture?"[26]

The Mission Coalition on Redevelopment (MCOR) narrowly defeated the Redevelopment Agency, saving the neighborhood from the destruction wrought in the Fillmore and South of Market districts. Their organizing model was more or less pulled from Saul Alinsky's playbook, establishing a formal membership and prioritizing moving established community leaders into their camp. This model departed from the Third World liberation discourse that would later influence the Mission District's other critical controversy—the trial of seven Latino youths in the shooting deaths of two police officers, known as the Los Siete de la Raza case.[27] The defense of Los Siete became a critical cause in the larger New Left and Latino politics of the time.

MCOR was able to unite disparate forces long enough to take advantage of ruptures in traditional liberal-conservative political coalitions. Eventually, MCOR became the Mission Coalition Organization (MCO), and enjoyed no small amount of political clout as Mayor Alioto funneled control of federal Model City money to the coalition.[28] Through this bloomed a massive array of social service and economic development organizations including the Mission Housing Development Corporation (MHDC), which would help found MAC years later.

It is undeniable that, in the United States, social movements usually have a hard time grappling with the spoils of short-term victories. When the money for housing and jobs is actually won, coalitions are tested over who administers and controls funds, sits on boards and commissions, and takes the credit. The rise of the nonprofit sector also mirrors the cross-ideological current in MCO. The pragmatic conservative can view a nonprofit housing developer as an agent of partial privatization. Some in the radical left would view the same entity as a chance to put into practice the politics of community control. The options are a few: abstain from organizing for reforms altogether, let others administer them while applying pressure from the outside, or try to maintain an authentic democratically controlled institution. No matter what the approach, the mere technical difficulty of administering development projects necessarily means at least a partial ceasefire with the state.

In the 1990s, these dynamics created antagonisms that ultimately pitted the old-school veterans of the space wars against a younger generation of Latino organizers. Mission Housing Development Corporation's staff people, particularly the firebrand organizer Eric Quezada, were central to the formation of MAC and were committed to bringing their own organization back to the tradition of organizing it had sprung from. MHDC's board of directors, on the other hand, felt that this shift endangered years of carefully cultivated insider clout that had produced thousands of affordable homes for the community. The MAC partisans, starting with Executive Director Carlos Ramirez, were fired. The board characterized the firings as an internal matter of disciplining workers who failed to follow protocol around political positions. Also central was the board's desire to build market-rate housing both inside and outside of the Mission. Without MHDC, MAC lost some credibility, as well as resources the other smaller organizations could not duplicate.[29]

### Creative Arts and Creative Protest: The Role of Art in the Mission

In the politics of gentrification, the role of the artist is an especially conflicted one. On one hand, artists (especially white ones) are used as the vanguard of gentrification. Their presence signifies that a neighborhood is a colorful alternative to the suburban greys. The majority of artists, voluntarily or not, are far from affluent, and few make a living from their art alone. Yet real estate interests are quick to promote artists as a sign that a neighborhood is in "transition" away from its dangerous origins toward an upscale future. In a sense, the position of artists in the displacement game reminds one of poor white laborers in the clearing of the West: once the frontier has been cleared and the natives subdued, so too must exit the bohemian.

In neighborhoods like the Mission, this is only part of the story—it assumes that all artists are white, déclassé, and from another part of the country. Many are, but the Mission District also has a long history of Latino arts with its own story—institutions like the Mission Cultural Center for Latino Arts and Galería de la Raza were part of a long tradition of cultural activism long before the displacement behemoth arrived in town. Despite their differences, white and brown artists alike face many of the same contradictions. They need cheap rent but also need to sell their work to survive, and usually it's to the same people who are driving up the rent.

Rebecca Solnit, writing in her important book *Hollow City: Gentrification and the Eviction of Urban Culture*, posits that artists are the weathervanes of gentrification since they need both cheap rent and a lot of space to develop their craft. The same can be said for the requirements to raise a family with limited means in a city. If a city has enough affordable space for everyone then it's easier for neighborhoods to nurture their own culture, and the impact of newcomers can be potentially enriching. Many artists see their fates as separate from other workers, even if thriving cultural conditions are in fact tethered to the overarching project of social justice. There is a tendency, even among socially engaged artists, to see themselves as above the fray of grassroots mobilization.

In the battle for the Mission District, a small group of artists showed that this didn't have to be the case. The San Francisco Print Collective's (SFPC) partnership with MAC set a standard for how artists can make themselves useful during times of political strife. While many other groups of artists spoke up only when their own art spaces were threatened with eviction, the SFPC collaborated with MAC to create brilliants silk-screened anti-gentrification posters promoting the struggles of the neighborhood. One poster in particular summed up the conflict with the slogan "They Plan for Profits, We Plan for People," over a picture of everyday people. The Print Collective listened to organizers and people in the neighborhood to develop messages of resistance and to publicize upcoming mobilizations. One SFPC artist, Eric Trillantafillou, insists that the group did not set out to subvert the role of artists in times of gentrification. "What the SFPC did was neither novel nor radical. We wanted to raise visibility about what was happening in our midst, and do it in and through a community-based social movement: the Mission Anti-Displacement Coalition. We believed that if something was going to change it could only happen through collective action oriented toward a set of specific aims, articulated through MAC. We were its autonomous propaganda wing. We made what we wanted, in support of MAC. I would say our work was instrumentalized in this sense, and that was a good thing. Politics is a means-ends game. We were playing politics with art."

## Soon the Rest Will Fall?

In 2000, the first dot-com gold rush was officially over as the majority of the new economy's superstars closed up shop. The thousands of square feet of office space pushed through to accommodate the boom went vacant, as did many of the contested live/work lofts. The market granted the neighborhood a stay of execution. Although rents dropped about 40 percent after the crash, the damage was already done. In the end, MAC was extremely successful in mounting a fight-back and curtailed the worst impacts of displacement, but even its innovative approach to organizing couldn't overcome both internal and external barriers.

The ballot box provided both strategic opportunities and a trap for anti-displacement activists. It would have been foolhardy for MAC to completely ignore the formal electoral and legislative channels for power. Decisions with real consequences for its constituencies were regularly made at the ballot box, in legislative chambers and city departments. The coalition also aspired to devolve decision making to the neighborhood level, through participatory planning processes. The decade presented several real opportunities to ameliorate displacement through legislative channels.

Inspired by the return of district-based elections, neighborhood groups fielded independent candidates to directly challenge the Board of Supervisors members installed by Mayor Brown.[30]

Electing supervisors by clusters of neighborhoods (instead of citywide) opened the door for populist candidates, particularly those without large financial backing viability. District elections were originally proposed in 1972 as part of a strategy of neighborhood organizations to bring political power to the neighborhoods. In 1977, the first district elections produced the city's first African-American, Asian, and openly gay supervisors. Blamed unfairly for the political acrimony that brought about the assassination of Harvey Milk in 1978, voters repealed district elections in 1980. This tilted the balance of power at the Board of Supervisors to the right—with the majority of supervisors favoring a Chamber of Commerce–backed development agenda. In 1996, the voters approved Proposition G, which reinstated district elections in time for the 2000 elections. After much internal debate, MAC decided to mobilize for candidates who could defeat Mayor Brown's loyalists on the board.

Of the eight candidates endorsed by MAC, seven were victorious, winning on platforms that were explicitly anti-displacement. One MAC coalition founder, Chris Daly, took District 6 (which included part of the Mission) by a landslide. Matt Gonzalez, a public defender and poetry patron, easily won the Haight and Western Addition after switching party affiliation from Democrat to Green in midstream. Gonzalez's victory fueled hopes that electoral alternatives to San Francisco's Democratic Party rule could be built. Proposition L, which encapsulated the spirit of MAC's planning demands, was defeated thanks to a large infusion of corporate cash and a decoy measure. L would have required the Planning Commission to take affordable housing, traffic, and small businesses into consideration when approving a development project. Proposition K, placed on the ballot by Mayor Brown, would have removed most of the remaining restrictions on high-tech office space. Voters rejected both measures.

After the progressive sweep at City Hall, participation in MAC fell even as the coalition began some of its most imaginative work: building a People's Plan (Plan Popular) as a way to intervene in the city's rezoning of the Mission under the Eastern Neighborhoods Plan. The People's Plan was developed, in part, through an eight-week process where residents were dropped into a local art gallery, viewed gigantic silk-screened maps of the neighborhood, and proposed their own ideas for development in their interests. While prefigurative and creative, MAC slowed the pace of street mobilization and direct action.

With the constellation of formal power temporarily bent leftward, this beat might have been remixed with delightful results. One SF Print Collective poster, cut in the shape of the a round bomb with a fuse sticking out of it, proclaimed, "The New Board of Supervisors is the Bomb, but the Voice of the People Is Much Louder." The movement had the potential to fight with both fists, grappling with realpolitik without becoming its captive. As it turned out, the populist side of the anti-displacement flame was doused as organiz-ers spent more and more time in City Hall. To be clear, the new Board of Supervisors passed pieces of legislation that (combined with the dot-com bust) slowed displacement and provided real bene-fits to working-class San Franciscans, but without the unpredictabil-ity of disruptive protest, progressive politicians had little reason to take risks that might have put their own careers in jeopardy.

"It wasn't that MAC stopped organizing, their work went on to about 2007 and they took on some of the most important develop-ment issues not just in the Mission, but the entire city," remarked Chris Daly. "It's just that so much of the energy went into mobilizing for meetings at City Hall, when in fact there was only so much that could get done there."

As MAC grappled with what its newfound access to power meant, it made a series of moves that curtailed a larger impact. Poor people's organizations in MAC had done a solid job making sure the voices of residential hotel tenants and day laborers were in the mix and that their campaigns were supported by the larger coalition. The nonprofits brought working-class people, particularly Latinos to the fold. This foundation helped to ground MAC's work to larg-er currents of international displacement, institutional racism, and persistent poverty. There was a fear, particularly among activists of color, that success would bury these dialogues beneath a race-blind populism, resulting in politics that would eventually exclude the very voices they had worked so hard to elevate. As MAC activist and Mis-sion Housing staffer Amie Fishman noted:

> MAC intentionally shifted its focus and turned inward to empower those traditionally marginalized—Latino immigrants, youth, SRO tenants, low-income families —to participate in the Mission's community-planning process. It was a challenge for MAC to retain its mass social movement and citywide character while focusing on the leadership development of its constituent base. Previously, when it achieved the former, progressive white activists, artists, and advocates were over-represented in MAC meetings and activities. When it aimed for the latter, there were few ways for people who were not affiliated with one of the

core member organizations to participate. Subsequently, with fewer large-scale mobilizations, partially due to the easing of external pressures after the dot-com boom busted and partially due to strategic choices, the grassroots leaders no longer had a movement to lead. It was then hard to sustain their involvement given the pressure of their daily lives and given the loss of movement energy.[31]

Many white residents bristled at the politics of self-determination, and accused nonprofit professionals of color of manipulating race and identity issues in order to centralize power and silence independent thought. Mission neighborhood organizing historically communicated movement goals around Latino terms, which was entirely justified given that it was not just physical homes at stake but a cultural home at well. In practice, MAC fought for reforms that would have benefited the vast majority of working-class residents but often stumbled when it came to articulating what a race-plus-class vision might look like. Traditional social movement tensions surfaced. It wasn't uncommon for meetings to be taken up with circular discussions of race and white advantages, which rarely evolved into a deeper shared politics and strategy.

At a MAC meeting in late 2001, the main organizations voted to establish a governance structure largely limited to their own ranks. The weekly meetings were eliminated, and the bulk of MAC's decisions were made during business hours. For those who were antagonistic toward nonprofit groups from the beginning, this action fulfilled their prophecy. At a pivotal moment in history, paid organizers responded to very real challenges with a fumble. Experimental new coalition structures could have simultaneously preserved MAC's success in reaching communities traditionally shut out of activist work and extended participation to those unaffiliated with an organization. The behavior of many (predominantly but not solely) white people only seemed to stoke fears that the politics of anti-displacement would be permanently whitewashed. Some sad examples: one longtime Green Party activist derided a Latina organizer as a "non-profit Pocohantas" after she expressed a difference of opinion with him; others insisted that any sort of talk of the whitening of the Mission

District was giving in to crass nationalism and would automatically kill the potential for a unified fight-back.

The debates around race and oppression in MAC mirrored the conflicts in the larger left. As Marti recalled, "There is a historic ideological divide among left activists between emphasizing an exclusively class-based or interest-based approach or an issue that affects particular communities. MAC tried to maintain an internationalist perspective, making alliances, and using particular cultural traditions as organizing strategies."

### Of Tactics and Strategies

The war for the neighborhood had been all-consuming. Evening meetings lasted until the early morning. Anonymous death threats (including a series of feces-stained, dada-esque cut-and-paste diatribes mailed to the Mission Agenda) were common, and the coalition had failed to fully resolve issues of how to exercise and maintain power.

MAC had made some good tactical moves. In an atmosphere heavy with race and class anxieties, it made a tactical alliance with (mostly white) artists and chose to focus most of its energies on developers and the politicians who enabled them. At certain points, activists who favored direct-action protests bumped up against others who feared that such tactics would place low-income community members in harm's way. This was resolved by a strategic ecumenicalism: direct action's partisans were allowed to up the ante with landlord visits, banner drops, and office occupations, which worked in tandem with traditional civil society tactics (flooding public comment at hearings, house meetings, and press conferences). For a period of time, it looked like MAC might become a living example of how to build a movement that could deploy the tactical preferences of its parts toward a common set of goals.

In his book *Local Protests, Global Movements: Capital, Community, and State in San Francisco*, author Karl Beitel asserts that "in the post-1970 period, urban actors have favored organizational forms that have afforded them the ability to act independently of political parties or party-like formations."[32] In MAC's case, this was simply not true. Most of the candidates backed by MAC were progressive Democrats and carried with them the baggage of their party. The political aspirations of most of MAC's key activists lay far beyond the ballot box, but a relentlessly pragmatic streak prevented a deeper practice of independence. The fact that at least four members had aspired to elected office (Eric Quezada, Chris Daly, Marc Salomon, and Renee Saucedo) was rarely interrogated in open discussion. Without such discussion, politics defaulted to its usual position: as a fence around a movement's potential.

MAC went against its own best instincts by over-relying on electoral and legislative politics to make an impact. What if progressive representatives were pushed further by neighborhood-wide or citywide rent strikes? What if the pace of landlord pickets increased after the sweep of Brown loyalists? What if the movement celebrated its electoral successes by opening new fronts of resistance, such as blocking sheriffs' evictions? Is it possible for a movement to fight with two fists? For people with very different ideas of where big change comes from to cooperate and leverage different tactics in a unified strategy? For a brief moment, MAC had the opportunity to find out and maybe forge new urban politics. That project is sadly unfinished.

One of the deepest contradictions in incremental neighborhood change is that both disinvestment and local improvements can fuel displacement. When a neighborhood is struggling with crime and vacancies (like the Mission did in the 1980s), speculators buy properties on the cheap and warehouse them to flip at a future point. Yet when grassroots organizations win needed improvements to transit, public space, and schools, in the absence of changes that protect the tenure of long-term residents, the neighborhood becomes more desirable. It's a nuance that should inform anti-displacement organizing in any city.

One of MAC's pillars, PODER has its roots in the environmental justice movement that arose in the late 1980s as an alternative to the racially blind approaches of mainstream environmentalists. The first PODER was formed by Antonio Diaz and others in Austin, Texas, and drew heavily from the pantheon of previous Latino-led political projects, such as the Brown Berets and the Central American solidarity movement. The first generation of the movement targeted polluting facilities located in working-class communities of color: Austin's PODER played a central role in closing a fuel tank farm that had caused illnesses in the community.

When Diaz came to San Francisco, the new PODER turned its attentions to the politics of the built environment, and their first organizing victory was winning a comprehensive lead-abatement ordinance. They won new parks for Mission District residents: the first won is city-controlled, and neighborhood residents have to pay to use the community center located on it—if they are lucky enough to still live nearby. PODER turned their attention to the elephant in the neighborhood: displacement. Largely thanks to Fair Housing regulations, much of the affordable housing located in the Mission can't directly be used to stop displacement. These regulations stipulate that most subsidized housing must administer a waiting list to gain tenancy, so, with few exceptions, the admissions process cannot prioritize those being displaced from a nearby building.

With this in mind, the choice to turn toward the city's planning process was a wise one. What other target could better illustrate the estrangement of long-term residents from the decisions impacting their lives? For MAC, the goal of rezoning the Mission was an excellent tactic—it would slow down development and give more opportunity to educate the public. This logical move wasn't an effective long-term strategy. Large changes in city planning were on the table, but they were ones rarely discussed in a global city (or in MAC for that matter) about what fundamental land reform could look like. It would have been possible, given MAC's strength at the time, to offer new visions of what community and public ownership could look like.

It's impossible to know exactly what could have kicked displacement to the curb in the 1990s. What is known is that the traditional arsenal of the anti-displacement activist was depleted. It was impossible to build affordable housing fast enough to replace what the market ate. Rent control remained important but far less effective in the face of rapid and resourceful gentrification. Big ideas, like amending the tax code to discourage speculation, or creating gentrification-proof bubbles of community-controlled housing, were marginalized. Respected affordable housing advocates active in MAC frequently spoke out against cooperative ownership and posed that zoning changes and more affordable housing would be enough to stem displacement.[33] Some cited real concerns that resourcing cooperatives would shift resources away from funding needed for nonprofit rental housing, which could serve lower-income households. Others simply thought that self-management models of housing were doomed to fail due to the complex nature of operating housing. MAC's ability to experiment with tactics didn't translate to an openness to newer strategies.

What MAC did accomplish was notable. They forced several private developers to provide more affordable housing than originally planned. Live-work lofts were placed under a moratorium that slowed the loss of important industrial space. MAC also raised expectations in San Francisco that urban development should benefit working communities. They also intervened in the war of ideas, insisting that displacement was the result of human choices, not natural outcomes of the market economy.

Diaz summed up the MAC experience: "When we were talking in the late nineties about the dot-com boom, it became obvious that the single-issue groups had to come together. Fighting gentrification wasn't going to be a short-term campaign. It would mean effective organizing, mass mobilizations, and more. MAC brought together groups that were already doing work and created a force that could counteract the displacement push."

"MAC had an impact because it meant that the Mission District community attempted to take control over its own destiny around critical issues such as housing and community planning. MAC created an optimism that you could fight and win," remarked Renee Saucedo, then director of the San Francisco Day Labor program, "Also, it was significant that immigrant day laborers, some of the most excluded members of society, participated."

Diaz has seen the limits of neighborhood organizing but still believes the local is the best place to begin to address the global. "There are no little utopias in capitalism," he explains. "We want to see massive public investment while simultaneously building local grassroots control."

## Tech-Fueled Displacement: Then and Now

In 2000, investors started to think twice about the tech boom. Perhaps realizing that few of the dot-com companies they had helped to create had actual business plans, investors sharply curtailed their contributions. Just a year before, 457 Bay Area tech companies started selling stock with initial public offerings (IPOs), but by the end of 2000, only seventy-six remained.[34] The shuttering of so much of tech's first wave sent many tech workers from the cocktail bar to the unemployment office. Many were driven into bankruptcy as a result of no longer being able to afford their mortgages or gigantic tax bills on worthless stock options.

Author and comedian Bucky Sinister worked at a Mission District tech company, Protazoa, in the late 1990s. The company specialized in motion capture technology used for animation in television and film. It was unique because it initially relied on real clients who paid bills to survive, instead of endless streams of venture capital. Sinister saw his income double in a year and waited for the company to go public so he could start selling stock for his big payoff.

Then the dot-com craze hit.

"The funding companies wanted to get in on it. The name was changed to Dotcomix. That was the beginning of the end of that place. The paying clients were dropped in favor of "gaining eyeballs." We were making cartoons for our own website. The problem was that most people didn't have an Internet connection capable of watching it. Few people had broadband back then," explained Sinister. Then as the financiers started to pull their money, Dotcomix shut its doors.

Sinister recalls the atmosphere of the dot-com era resembling a late-twentieth century version of *The Great Gatsby* "Drugs, drinking, cab rides, dining out: people spent everything they made on $12 cocktails. Other people bought houses and cars, but they couldn't pay them off once everything crashed. If you worked in the dot-com industry, you could have anything financed. But suddenly, the company was gone. I was fucked. I was making $250 a week on unemployment, but I couldn't meet minimum payments for everything, and the credit cards maxed out, and then they extended my credit so I could owe more interest and fees. There were late fees and interest compounding every month. I was unemployed for nine months."

Stories like these lead some to opine that the solution to displacement is to wait for the market to correct itself. Twitter and Facebook stock have both been remarkably volatile. While today's tech might

75

not maintain its current breakneck pace, hopes for a correction are sadly overblown. Tech 2.0 is heavily integrated into everyday business, communications, and surveillance industries.

As we will see in the next two chapters, solving the housing crisis means shifting toward stewardship and away from purely market-based panaceas, instead of waiting for a crash that might never happen. If history is any indicator, if another crash visits San Francisco, at best it will be a quick break in the displacement saga.

## Chapter Four
## A Shift toward Stewardship:
## Is the Displacement War Over, If We Want It to Be?

**2001.** The San Francisco Community Land Trust was founded on a basic question: *what if we could win the housing war?*

San Francisco had seen skilled organizing to defeat evictions, only to have new evictions filed in the same buildings a few years later. Housing occupations rarely had the lasting impact of the actions that forced the Housing Authority to open 250 vacant units. State law curtailed the potential power of rent control. If housing remained in the market, then it would eventually be lost to the market.

A community land trust (CLT) is a form of social housing in which the residents cooperatively own their building but are sewn into a larger community-controlled organization, which owns the land below. Through resale restrictions and ongoing resident education, homes are affordable forever. The land trust helps residents develop the skills of self-management and participatory governance. This arrangement not only protects the interests of residents, but also those of the larger community of people who need housing.

As defined by land trust pioneer John Emmeus Davis, a land trust is distinct from other forms of social ownership in four major ways:

- Land is treated as a common heritage, not as an individual possession. Title to multiple parcels is held by a single not-for-profit, which manages these lands on behalf of a particular community, present and future.
- Land is removed permanently from the market, never resold. Land is put to use, however, by leasing out individual parcels for the construction of housing, the production of food, the development of commercial enterprises, or the promotion of other activities that support individual livelihood or community life.
- All structural improvements are owned separately from the land, with title to these buildings held by individual homeowners, business owners, housing cooperatives, or the owners of any other buildings located on leased land.

- A ground lease lasting many [usually ninety-nine] years gives owners of these structural improvements the exclusive use of land beneath their buildings, securing their individual interests while protecting the interests of the larger community.[1]

Nationally, there are about 190 land trusts, with approximately 6,500 homes, which is less than .005 percent of the total amount of households in the United States. Over the past decade, the land trust has become an aspiration in anti-displacement fights, with activists establishing new organizations in Chicago, New York, Florida, and Los Angeles. Part of its popularity can be attributed to the fact that it can be seen through multiple lenses: on one hand, it has characteristics associated with progressive sympathies—affordability, community control, and land reform. On the other, it is also firmly a form of homeownership with protections largely agreed upon through private contracts, instead of government regulation.

In order to appreciate the potential of CLTs let's revisit the 1990s Mission District and imagine what could have been different if a robust community-ownership strategy had been fully implemented. In reality, protests of elderly Lola McKay's eviction led to a small reform: landlords evicting tenants under the Ellis Act had to provide sixty days' notice instead of only thirty. Let's say that the occupation, instead of fizzling out, had attracted many thousands of people to the offices of the landlord's attorney, and that the protest lasted weeks, not hours. And that this, in turn, catalyzed a wave of direct actions—sheriffs' evictions were successfully blocked, courtroom proceedings were packed with supporters of the evictees. Landlords, fearing retribution, would quietly recall eviction notices.

In this alternative future, let's imagine that a portion of San Francisco's housing movement sought and gained power through the ballot box, just as they did in reality. Many fear that the election of a nominally progressive Board of Supervisors will ultimately serve to demobilize a movement; others are concerned with the capacity of the housing movement to continue through a direct-action-only strategy. Instead of launching into polemics against each other, the two camps arrive at an inside-outside strategy. Direct action will be used to prevent and confront evictions. In addition, outside organizers agree to continually demand more than whatever their counterparts in City Hall put forward as solutions.

Those who prefer public-policy advocacy and working within City Hall begin working on the infrastructure for a citywide CLT that is capable of helping residents convert their properties to permanently affordable, self-managed housing. The CLT is funded through progressive taxation on commercial real estate and pension fund investments from local trade unions. Now, when landlords want to evict, they are mandated to give existing tenants the right of first refusal to (collectively) purchase their own homes.

At first, the land trust acquires a single building, a twenty-unit apartment in the heart of the Mission District. This building was the site of a massive rent strike and occupation that forced the landlord to sell. Over the course of the next few years, the CLT effectively becomes the engine for the decommodification of five hundred units and is also working with traditional nonprofit housing providers to add additional rental stock for those who prefer to not live cooperatively. Gradually, a new map of the Mission and the larger San Francisco area shows gentrification-proof bubbles. Residents, not worried about the future of their housing, can consider how they would like their neighborhood to be developed. The resident associations, built with the CLT's help, aid a project of decentralized participatory neighborhood democracy. It is no longer possible for developers to sell harmful projects under the cover of more jobs. Likewise, residents do develop their neighborhoods, building economic opportunities such as worker-owned cooperatives and strong local-hire arrangements. Small landlords, already existing, are allowed to remain in business and even make a reasonable living at it as long as they refrain from evicting tenants for profit and maintain their buildings.

### Looking for a Way out of the Housing Crisis

The initial group of people who came together to form the San Francisco Community Land Trust (SFCLT) varied in their backgrounds and politics. They included an anarchist architect from Uruguay, a local activist with a vendetta against existing nonprofit community development corporations, several public aid recipients, urban planning students, a dissident capitalist developer, and several union workers. All supported rent control protections but were painfully aware of their limitations. As we saw in Chapter 4, San Francisco's Rent Arbitration and Stabilization Ordinance of 1979 was cut off at the knees, thanks to state law prohibiting vacancy control, and the Ellis Act. And as long as housing remained in the speculative market, the forces of displacement would eventually win, even if organizers routinely leveraged relocation benefits or were able to substantially delay evictions.

Most of the existing nonprofit developers who were dedicated to building new units of affordable housing were unable to stabilize existing communities. Nonprofit housing organizations prefer an economy of scale—developing at least a hundred units. Just like buying organic food in bulk, this drives the overall unit price downward. It makes it easier to provide housing for lower-income people and make scarce funding more efficient. But the bulk of the evictions were happening in the mid-sized buildings—too small to be considered for conversion to traditional affordable housing. This was the old housing social contract: build new construction and let rent control stabilize the rest of the housing market. This was strategy worked from the 1970s until the early 1990s but had met its limits. With landlords and speculators rushing to turn their buildings into condominiums, fueling speculative evictions, the SFCLT felt it was urgent to create a new form of community ownership that would beat back the displacement monster. A CLT could provide completely legal vacancy control and preserve affordable housing in perpetuity. It was a bigger weapon in the fight against displacement.

The SFCLT arrived at a governance structure common to most land trusts:

- The land trust would be a membership organization; any resident of San Francisco who agreed with our principles could join and vote.
- The majority of the board of directors would be directly elected by the membership.
- Changes to bylaws would have to be approved at general membership meetings, not simply by vote of the board of directors.

## The Fight for the Fong Building

Taking housing off the speculative market in one of the most expensive cities in the world is a gigantic task. For the San Francisco Land Trust it meant learning to translate organizing "demands" into the creation of a counter-institution; activists no longer had the luxury of simply critiquing other approaches to the housing crises. Providing housing also meant learning the basics of finance, traditional management, and how to engage local government. We had to create a basic system for this. We couldn't simply insist that evictions cease. We had to figure out ways to finance cooperative conversions but build reserves for future repairs. As difficult as these things are under the best of circumstances, they were, at least theoretically, possible in the absence of a landlord who expected windfall profits.

The land trust made several mistakes in its infancy. One of the most glaring was designing a piece of legislation to convert rental housing to cooperative housing without having specific projects to apply these ideas to. The proposal, if enacted, would have enabled the conversion of many hundreds of rental units before adequate procedures were in place to ensure that speculators couldn't find a loophole. This resulted in a lot of unneeded friction with the very people we considered respected comrades, such as the San Francisco Tenants Union, who were fighting off many landlord-funded assaults on rent control masquerading as first-time home buyer opportunities, at the time.

Inordinate amounts of time were spent on a city created Community Land Trust Taskforce. The task force was officially charged with finding ways to grow CLTs in San Francisco. Instead it became a venue for city officials to undermine the idea of a land trust and some land trust partisans to fire off polemics against the sins of existing nonprofit developers. It was a mistake to turn to the government for permission before developing a clear vision of what we wanted as an organization. Rene Casenave, a veteran housing organizer, gave the land trust the best advice ever: "Find some people to be useful to, find a building that needs saving, then work out all the legal shit."

Turns out that those people weren't hard to find. The SFCLT's first building was the Fong Building in San Francisco's Chinatown, 53 Columbus Avenue, just around the corner from the site of the

International Hotel struggle and a block from the Transamerica Building. The Fong Building's story starts off like most displacement dramas: someone buys a building and decides that its "highest and best use" doesn't include the tenants who have lived there for decades.[2] The building's immigrant tenants, families, seniors, and disabled people look at their gentrifying city and expect that they too will join the exodus out of town.

Usually the story ends soon thereafter. Eviction day comes, and people leave. Some find new homes in working-class suburbs that may turn into hot real estate years later, others move in with relatives, and a few end up sleeping in a homeless shelter. Every once in awhile, the story ends with just a little less sadness: tenants protest or sue and leverage a better buyout plan. In either situation, the fabric of a community, the basis of the true resources that lie beyond both the market and the state, is lost. Gone are the ways that people check in on elderly neighbors when they return from work. Vanished are the quiet acts of mutual aid that help people survive: a loan until payday, a phone call saying that your kids are playing in the street too close to traffic. Academics and professional planners rarely attempt to quantify kindness—let alone uphold it as part of the global city.

But the residents of 53 Columbus wrote a remarkably different story. When they were told in 1998 that City College of San Francisco planned to evict them to build a new campus on their building's land, the mostly monolingual, Chinese-speaking residents dug in and fought back. Combining the legal prowess of the Asian Law Caucus with the community organizing of Chinatown Community Development Center, the tenants protested, picketed, and sued their way to a result far better than any buyout plan.

In 2006, the SFCLT bought the building from San Francisco City College, starting a five-year process of renovating the distressed property and turning it into a cooperative. Forcing the college to sell the building to the community and winning the funds to pay for it were the result of a multi-pronged strategy, the first element of which was tenant mobilization. Tenants picketed the college and mobilized for hearings at City Hall. Protests challenged City College's narrative that the displacement was simply a small inconvenience toward the larger goal of the college being able to better serve the Chinese community. They also provided political leverage for a sympathetic district supervisor, Aaron Peskin to push forward height restrictions that made it difficult, if not impossible, to develop the site as the tower envisioned by City College. He used strong-arm tactics to pass legislation that restricted the height limits only for that parcel and the adjacent one. Land trust activists played a bluff card by showing up at the Department of Elections and taking out papers to oppose City College's construction-bond initiative under the name "Campaign to Oppose City College's No-Good, Very Bad Waste of Tax Payer's Money." There was no capacity to run an electoral campaign, but it caused journalists to call Chancellor Phillip Day and ask if he felt threatened by the initiative.

Temporarily stymied, City College attempted to sell the building to a major developer who made off-the-cuff comments at public events that he would demolish the building. The Asian Law Caucus filed suit, citing a law that state-chartered community colleges have to give first preference to nonprofit entities when disposing of public property. After learning that the building would be extremely vulnerable in the event of a major earthquake, the Asian Law Caucus convinced the city of San Francisco to use seismic-stabilization funds, left over from the response to the 1989 Loma Prieta earthquake to purchase the building. The SFCLT purchased the building and began a multi-year renovation project, turning a dilapidated building into beautiful homes and an increased community space.

Many of the events leading to this victory seem, at first glance, to be insider politics. Granted, the legal and City Hall maneuvering was critical—it would not have been possible to force the sale of the building to the nonprofit before the private investor without the lawsuit filed by the Asian Law Caucus. However, none of this would have been possible without crucial choices made by the tenants. In one case, the elders in the building were offered generous relocation packages, which were denied to the younger families. They flatly refused. Five years later, the Fong Building was renamed Columbus United Cooperative by the residents.

The SFCLT's application of the land trust model to resident-occupied housing diverged from the majority of other trusts in the country. Most other trusts built new housing or specialized in reclamation of abandoned and vacant properties—both approaches are useful to combat displacement.

Gentrification doesn't happen all at once. More often than not, the first phase is disinvestment, when high vacancies and deindustrialization lead to low land prices. Eventually, developers, recognizing the future value of the land, buy up property cheap and warehouse it for years until the time is right to flip it.[3] While there are many variables and differences between cities, there are a few major markers in the process of displacement. Following disinvestment comes rebranding, as a neighborhood is marketed as "up and coming" with potential for profits and cultural appeal. The rebranding process is complex because it requires an act of spatial amnesia (forgetting and marginalizing the history of the neighborhood) and cultural fetishization (selective memory and celebration of the non-threatening aspects of the other). This is where the real estate industry gets to tell its story, providing an ideology that allows individuals to divest themselves from the consequences of displacement around them. It is the wink and the nudge to potential investors that says this frontier will be cleared. The final phase is hyper-investment, which comes both in the form of private finance and public-infrastructure improvements. The strength of the CLT model is that it can intervene at various moments in the lifecycle of a neighborhood.

SFCLT's strategy was to intervene at the point of eviction, using a variety of political tactics to force the sale price downward and to leverage necessary public resources for repairs. Other land trusts, such as Boston's Dudley Street Neighborhood Initiative and Albuquerque's Sawmill Community Land Trust were formed when the market was cooler—allowing a preemptive strike against displacement. One of the strengths of the land trust model is that it can be both a crisis-intervention model, to prevent displacement, and a tool to provide communities with real community-planning power.

The Sawmill Community Land Trust is as much an environmental justice project as it is a housing-development initiative. It was founded in the 1990s, when residents feared that the displacement and rent hikes in nearby neighborhoods would soon reach their own. A traditionally Latino neighborhood, Sawmill had massive vacant tracts of housing, many of them polluted by the detritus of the departed

particleboard company. After convincing city government to help finance the purchase of twenty-seven acres, Sawmill now hosts several
land trust buildings, as well as low-income rental housing for seniors.

The power of eminent domain ravaged communities of color in
the rrban renewal pushes of 1960s and 1970s. One set of activists,
the Dudley Street Neighborhood Initiative (DSNI), gambled that
eminent domain could be utilized to preserve community. Boston's
Dudley neighborhood was a poster child for abandonment for most
of the 1980s, but as part of a local campaign of development without
displacement the organization successfully pushed the city to vest the
power of eminent domain in it. DSNI has built hundreds of units on
abandoned land, as well as community centers, open space, and small
businesses.

Casas del Pueblo is a new Chicago land trust initiative that aims
to meet the housing needs of low-income families by pressuring
banks to turn over foreclosed properties to residents. Several homes
owned by Fannie Mae and Freddie Mac have been occupied by families who likely would face homelessness otherwise. Confronted with
community pressure, the banks often agreed to stall evictions during
negotiations.

One of the faces of Chicago's eviction crisis is Sabrina Morey, a
mother whose landlord was being foreclosed on. Morey got involved,
and helped organize with her landlord, only to be evicted after the
loan was modified. "That experience taught me that poor families
need to have their own land in order to survive and improve their
lives. I helped my landlord fight her eviction, but in the end I was
still on her property."

What is going on in Chicago reflects an evolving understanding
of occupations as a tactic in a larger strategy of building community
ownership and the removal of housing from the speculative market. As Holly Krig, a member of Casas del Pueblo, remarked, "The
conversation about the land trust then becomes a very important
education and organizing tool, as it is an opportunity to think about
what housing as a human right might actually look like. It's a way
to get past the talk of principle reductions or modifications and all
that shit that does nothing to challenge the underlying issues—privatization, capitalism."

The demands of Casas are simple: the banks should sell the homes to the community for a dollar, and residents should run the buildings with their neighbors with minimum bureaucratic interference. Organizing largely within the Latino community, their politics echo Zapata's claim *La tierra es de quien la trabaja con sus propias manos* (the land belongs to those who work it with their hands). They point out that the occupations have already created value by keeping the homes inhabited and in good repair.

Casas's approach is equal parts bolt cutters and financial planning. Though they have not yet secured a building, they have already achieved what seemed unthinkable just a few years ago, by halting foreclosures. "When I think of community control, I think of a community that is able to plan its own future because they are not having to struggle so much just to *stay*. We know what we want. We want to live in dignity and have the resources we need close by, just like in richer people's neighborhoods. But I don't see that happening unless we have some security, and that can't happen if we can be evicted easily. That's why we the takeovers and occupations are our tactics to build a movement towards the basic human right of housing."

In Manhattan, an effort to house homeless people is poised to create a land trust that could have an impact well beyond the ranks of the unhoused. In 2010, Picture the Homeless (PTH) gathered nearly 12,000 addresses of vacant buildings from Freedom of Information Act requests submitted to eighteen different city agencies. Bringing together homeless people, urban planning students, and community volunteers, PTH found enough housing and vacant lots to house 199,981 people.[4] The organization led a direct-action campaign to force the city to institutionalize housing counts and begin the process of converting vacant property into viable housing.[5] PTH members studied alternative housing models and became fascinated with the land trust as a method of providing both affordable housing and community control. Through this process, they learned that several other organizations were exploring land trusts as an option, and the New York City Community Land Initiative was born. With over thirty member organizations, the initiative is fighting to recycle housing that would have otherwise been wasted before it was eventually seized for private development.

Sam Miller, a housing organizer with PTH, hopes that within a short period of time, new cooperatives will bloom in Harlem, a neighborhood facing sharp displacement pressures. There have also been overtures from Hurricane Sandy survivors on Staten Island who want to use the land trust model as a collective-bargaining tool with FEMA and local government. PTH is using the opportunity to start a conversation about what housing for all looks like, as many people interested in the model carry with them anxieties that the crime rate will increase with the inclusion of formerly homeless people in the mix. "We often think about all of the good things that community means, and forget that community can also be really exclusive and xenophobic as well." In that sense, land isn't the only thing that will be held in trust. Miller hopes that the process will help build trust and solidarity between communities often pitted against each other.

## The Radical Roots of Community Land Trusts

The land srust's roots run back well over a century and are firmly in the tradition of American utopian communalism. In 1879, writer Henry George asked in *Progress and Poverty* how intense poverty could exist next to extreme opulence. Where Karl Marx pointed the finger at the ownership of the means of production, George blamed the concentration of ownership of land as the root cause of poverty. George was highly influenced by John Stuart Mill's idea of a "social increment," that the value of land appreciates largely because of the growth and development of society instead of labor power or capital investment. George cast landlords as unproductive leeches who would siphon off, through higher rents, the potential of economic progress to benefit the mass of people. George recommended taxing away the social increment to pay for social needs—from schools to infrastructure and services.

George's theories are easy to critique because he dismisses the inputs that build the social increment, namely capital accumulation and human wage-labor. From another vantage point, he is also an early proponent of spatial politics—recognizing the power relations that shape the city and the people who live in it. George, writing from San Francisco in the 1870s, witnessed a city quickly urbanizing to changes in global capital. The Pacific Stock Exchange opened in

1878, followed by the completion of the Southern Pacific Railroad, which connected Los Angeles and San Francisco. Those influenced by George developed wild proposals for alternative urban spaces. One such follower, Ebenezer Howard, dreamed of creating garden cities, which would be developed on land leased from a municipal corporation. Howard had a role in directly developing thirty-two garden cities in England, while others developed similar cities in Delaware and Alabama.[6]

In the 1920s and 1930s, Communist Party USA stalwarts attempted a grand experiment of cooperative housing in New York City. Founding the United Workers Cooperative in the Bronx, the development welcomed black residents and developed libraries, worker-owned businesses, and youth clubs. Subsequent Communist-backed cooperatives included the Farband Houses, Shalom Alecich, and the Amalgamated Houses, founded by the garment workers' union.[7] The land trust's approach of balancing the self-management of existing tenants against the right to housing of future generations evolved in response to this experiment. Many of the Red Cooperatives had stand-alone governance structures, meaning that decisions were made on a one-vote-per-household basis. While seemingly democratic, this approach allowed affordability restrictions to be removed by majority vote of the residents. This is exactly what happened as revolutionary idealism waned over the decades.

In 1968, one of the first community land trusts in the United States was established in southwestern Georgia as a strategy for building a foundation for black political action. The New Communities initiative occupies thousands of acres of rural land and is a lesser-known project of the civil rights era. Founder Charles Sherrod began contemplating the land question while a young organizer with the Student Nonviolent Coordinating Committee (SNCC) and doing door-to-door organizing against southern Jim Crow laws.

> I guess the thing that prompted me to think in terms of self-sustaining capacity more than anything else was knocking on doors all over the country—whether it was in Mississippi, Alabama, Georgia, or in Virginia where I was born. I was hearing people say the same thing time and time again. "What you going

to do if I get kicked out of my house? You young people are talking a good talk—this is a good thing you're doing—but I live on this man's land, and what am I going to do if they take my job, my house? What am I going to do with my children?"

This was when I was organizing in the field and that was a resounding echo in my mind for years and years, a question I was never able to answer: Who shoulders responsibility when it happens? It wasn't as if it was a hollow question, because right there before my eyes every year were examples of people losing their jobs and all security, contracts dishonored, children not being able to eat. So what could I do? There they were. And there I was—with my commitment, but no power; my love but no bread. And with all my tenacity and strength of mind, I couldn't employ nobody. So years of that—on dusty roads, thinking and talking riding through and looking at people's homes on plantations, getting kicked off plantations myself, periling other people's houses and sustenance myself, just being on their plantation. The only solution that one could come to would be that we have to own the land ourselves.[8]

New Communities survived until the mid-1980s, when a severe southern drought crippled the cooperatives' economic base of farming. The US Department of Agriculture, which routinely approved emergency loans of irrigation systems to white farmers, denied New Communities the same protection.

### The New Housing Common Sense

A stark reading of the banking industry's own numbers paints a picture of the failure of the real estate system to provide safe, decent, and affordable housing for all. According to the Mortgage Bankers Association, one in about two hundred homes has been foreclosed upon, and every three months, 250,000 families enter into foreclosure.[9] The American Dream builds a willingness to accept this state of affairs even though it has failed so many. Outside of the funding needed to acquire property, one of the most pressing needs of the land trust movement is that it develop the capacity to challenge what Americans expect from their housing—housing as a personal investment and direct wealth creator. No matter how quickly the CLT movement evolves, it can be useful in building a new common sense around housing and urban living. Building such sense is rarely direct, and it relies on the cultivation of many messages over many decades to imbed it. If asked directly, few people would endorse the idea that foreclosures and evictions are positives for society. Laissez faire private-property arrangements need ideological acrobatics to achieve broad appeal. During the conquest, notions of a Christian mission fueled the landgrabs and genocide that many would have been reticent to take part in otherwise. Likewise, the push toward single-family suburban home ownership wasn't merely a feat of freeways and GI Bills: the ideological story was told of a nuclear family, economic success, and rugged individualism. Not far beneath the surface was another undergirding story—that of racism, white flight, and a fear of a city.

A land trust goes against the American grain of individual ownership as a sacred right and only final solution to the housing crisis. The ethic of stewardship replaces the profit motive, and under that ethic, the highest and best use of land is measured by shared social gains, equitable economic development, and protection of community from the fluctuations of the market. It is impossible to know if CLTs will ever transcend their small role in the United States and grow to scale. CLTs are asked to provide safe, decent, and affordable housing, prevent displacement, and somehow also perform as a laboratory for participatory democracy *and* self-determination. It's difficult enough to do just one of the things on this list well, let alone stay connected to a larger movement to challenge the capitalist vision of the city.

## Challenges for the Community Land Trust Movement

As traditional approaches to housing stabilization reach their limits, the community land trust movement is in a good position to grow in size and influence. Even before the foreclosure crisis of 2008, many cities held thousands of vacant homes. This is a crucial moment for serious national land-reform movements. As the CLT movement grows, CLTs will likely face many of the same challenges that nonprofit community development corporations have faced for several decades. Utopian aspirations are easily attached to the idea of a land trust. The communitarian ethos and radical traditions can lead some of its partisans to elevate it above all other solutions. There is also a tendency, common throughout many cooperative experiments, to divorce rather than engage the larger movements for the right to the city. It is important that land trusts be viewed as a sneak preview of a better world instead of a utopia on a single city block.

Paying attention to the complicated aspects of self-management's mechanics is a political act. If land trusts fall into disrepair or succumb to infighting they lose their most powerful element as an example of what can be. To avoid this, they must carefully develop the skills of residents to carry out the tasks usually reserved by property management professionals. Developing building operating and replacement reserves, stewarding public investment, and mediating conflict should never be shoved aside as secondary aims. Every failed or distressed cooperative builds a case that housing's only providers are either found in the marketplace or within the realm of traditional nonprofits. The utopian impulse may be the inspiration, but it is only made possible through hard work and attention to details.

The considerable technical demands of running desirable housing, complying with funders and regulation, will always compete with aspirations to build a housing movement. The land trust movement's history brings with it a commitment to address housing needs, structural racism, and inequality. Land trust activists must have a commitment to infusing their organizations with these values. It is important to demonstrate that land trusts are part of a viable housing strategy, while at the same time tethering them to the social movements that often give birth to them.

A technically proficient CLT runs safe, decent, and permanently affordable housing. This is a building block of a the land trust movement's ability to be a credible player in the large movement for social justice in the city. Rhetoric around decommodification and upholding the right to the city means nothing if existing CLTs are in a perpetual crisis of habitability and poor management. For some CLTs, this means challenging purist notions of what self-management looks like. In the early days of the San Francisco CLT, activists argued that working-class renters were largely managing their own buildings—doing repairs, resolving conflicts, and making payments. Following this logic, they assumed that all that was needed was the autonomy provided by community ownership. This ended up being a grand miscalculation. While the ability to self-manage is certainly within reach of all tenants, it doesn't magically appear and empower residents to grapple with the complexities of property stewardship. Without a strong outside displacement threat, some residents become antagonistic to a land trust and to their neighbors. This has resulted in the land trust becoming much more intentional in the way it develops skills, seeing self-management as a process instead of a given.

Despite some land trust activists' reticence to engage the state, the reality is that even the occasional donated property requires capital to maintain. CLTs are a significant step toward the decommodification of housing but can't solve the crisis alone. In the absence of truly radical change, land trusts will have to relate to and engage the state. It's best to think of the approach as a transitional program leading toward a humane housing sector, rather than as the final solution.

A land trust without the community in it is a neutral entity. It can be used for just about any purpose, including the maintenance of existing social advantages. For example, cities often have municipal land trusts to promote market-rate housing or commercial development, such as malls. Additionally, some early housing cooperatives have devolved away from founding egalitarian values toward racially discriminatory practices. The land trust model offers one structural safeguard over the stand-alone cooperative's ability to become exclusive. Through the split governance structure of the board of directors, the interests of those in the larger community who need stable housing are balanced against those who already have found it through the CLT. Organizational commitments toward political education and equitable distribution of its homes are critical. However, it is the almost intangible (and immeasurable) sense that one is part of a project much more important than short-term self-interest that may be the best safeguard against parochialism. Land trusts should actively encourage their residents to support important struggles in their cities, whether related to housing, immigration, racial justice, or more global concerns.[10]

A social-justice-oriented CLT remains a part of the broader struggle for the right to the city, as it is not satisfied with only providing housing. The politics of anti-displacement and human rights must be welded into CLTs' governing documents and promoted by volunteers, staff, and board. CLTs should develop concrete ways of assessing conversion opportunities and vetting inevitable potential compromises.

Landgrabs and Lies: images from the North Beach public housing struggle.
Credit: James Tracy.

Slow burn: images from the residential hotel struggles. Credit: James Tracy.

Slow burn: images from the residential hotel struggles. Credit: top, James Tracy; bottom, Coalition on Homelessness.

They Plan for Profits, We Plan for People: images from the Mission Anti-Displacement Coalition. Credits: top, Pancho Alatorre; bottom, Pedro Rios.

They Plan for Profits, We Plan for People: images from the Mission Anti-Displacement Coalition. Credits: top, SF Print Collective; bottom, Fernando Martí.

They Plan for Profits, We Plan for People: images from the Mission Anti-Displacement Coalition. Credits: top, MAC; bottom left, Peter Cohen; bottom right, SF Print Collective.

They Plan for Profits, We Plan for People: images from the Mission Anti-Displacement Coalition. Credits: SF Print Collective.

**They Plan for Profits, We Plan for People: images from the Mission Anti-Displacement Coalition. Credits: SF Print Collective.**

They Plan for Profits, We Plan for People: images from the Mission Anti-Displacement Coalition. Credits: SF Print Collective.

A Shift Toward Stewardship: images from the struggle to turn 53 Columbus into a community land trust co-op. Credits: top, Fernando Martí, bottom, Malcolm Yeung.

# Chapter Five
## Toward an Alternative Urbanism

**July 2014.** If the goal of an anti-displacement movement is to stop displacement, then San Francisco's movement has failed by any stretch of the imagination. San Francisco today is an exclusive city; what remains of working-class and artistic life there is on the ropes. Thankfully a total knockout cannot be called in this round. Organizations such as Eviction Free San Francisco have resuscitated the art of disruptive action in confronting displacement. Their creative blockades of the "Google Buses," the private charter buses shuttling well-paid tech workers to and from their jobs outside San Francisco, have once again put displacement in the international media. Visits to evicting landlords, and the industries that support them, are a weekly occurrence. Several promising populist electoral fights are on the horizon. Initiatives to curb property speculation by taxing away the profits made from quick flipping of properties are remarkable in that they show a willingness to address the roots of the problem. If, in a few years, part of San Francisco's soul remains intact it will be because of these campaigns and other people and organizations willing to dig deep, learn from past mistakes, and create a space for independent politics. Several lessons from the experiences of San Francisco's communities who fought in the 1990s are instructive today.

The very notion of the commons, of resources provided outside of the market, is tied to society's perception of race, class, and gender. Specifically, commons (and reforms) are created at the intersection of the aspirations of social movements to expand popular power and the desires of elites to contain popular protests. It is this contradiction that shapes social progress and reform in any given era. Therefore, to defend public housing means simultaneously fighting for the human right of housing, while refusing to embrace politics that flatten out the historical bigotries and exclusions in the name of unity.

Federal housing policy has been used to control and contain black Americans, often to accelerate the profit accumulation of urban-development regimes. At times, this is meticulously planned; at others it is a product of opportunism. In either situation, the conditions that black people live in are generally a good indicator of what is in store for the general population. In reality, what happened to public housing residents—particularly black residents—was the canary in the housing-crisis coal mine. For example, "Self-Sufficiency Specialists," employed by the Housing Authority, aggressively identified the most stable families in the developments, those with steady, if low-wage employment. These families were offered home ownership opportunities if they "cashed out" Section 8 vouchers, risking future housing assistance. The devil was in the details. Potential home buyers were often sold risky loan products, such as adjustable-rate and interest-only mortgages. The homeownership opportunities they were offered were often in working-class suburbs. Fast forward to 2008: many of these same families fell victim to foreclosure as housing payments skyrocketed. Yet again, corporate- and government-housing policies colluded to displace black people and to provide a template by which other communities were also displaced.[1]

Those who favor austerity and privatization have a reliable formula for their success. First, starve public resources, so that they can't possibly succeed; next, point to the pathologies, corruption, and contradictions of public resources that are sure to flourish under conditions of neglect. When HOPE VI was first proposed, many residents rightfully were enthusiastic, thinking that their developments would finally be fit for human habitation. Of course, the ultimate fate of the buildings themselves was never in question. Organizers, both residents and outside collaborators, excelled at putting forth a nuts-and-bolts right-to-return exit contract, based on basic understandings of human rights. What we never fully understood was the right to return to *what*? That left residents very receptive to the Housing Authority's message that HOPE VI would be a panacea for crime, joblessness, and poverty. By the time the majority of the residents recognized the need to act to secure their homes, the die had been cast.

Residents of San Francisco's North Beach had developed their own plan for self-management of their rebuilt development. While the outside collaborators agreed with the spirit of what was called the "Human Technologies" plan, we had serious reservations about their collaboration with a mysterious Florida-based developer who had little track record. That meant we gave lip service to the spirit of the plan but didn't speak up about its deficiencies. This was a mixed opportunity to expand the conversation about what revitalization from below could really look like—a situation where residents wouldn't have to bet housing security against jobs and community safety. While I believe that we were probably correct about Human Technologies, we should have fought harder and demanded that the residents be given the resources and technical support to bring their vision of democratic self-management forward.

The organizations that came together to support public housing residents in the HOPE VI process had many of the qualities of great organizers. We were relentlessly independent, extremely clear and principled in our politics, and willing to put in the long volunteer hours required to win. What we didn't fully grapple with was the reality that a hundred-million-dollar-plus development project creates its own set of friends—developers, trade unions, service organizations, and politicians. While we won important victories, we overestimated (perhaps romanticized) the ability of poor people and all-volunteer (broke) organizations to influence the process. Beyond calling for more direct action, we didn't have much of a plan about how to bridge the power-and-influence gap between us and our opponents. To be fair to us, many of the organizations we should have made common cause with were not interested in challenging Mayor Brown and his allies alongside such a rag tag coalition. Those who did (like the Asian Law Caucus, Chinatown Community Development Center, and Bay Area Legal Aid) did so out of a long-term commitment to poor people.

One of the biggest ironies about our organizing is that we could be so ecumenical and sectarian at the same time. We were willing to believe in the power and intelligence of the forgotten and excluded of San Francisco—public housing residents. Yet we also came across as extremely hard to work with to the few organizations willing to risk Mayor Brown's ire, even if we didn't think they were "radical" enough. We were quick to call sellout, and slow to think through what it takes to build a strong coalition. We never really did much to link up with other residents of other HOPE VI developments or other forms of federally subsidized housing. For all of the local collaboration, the basic agenda of HOPE VI was determined in Washington. Beyond a short-lived attempt to link up with Chicago's Cabrini-Green residents, this approach never materialized.

Many of the same dynamics were evident in the campaigns to preserve SRO hotels. In the late 1990s, the Mission Agenda was not the only organization in San Francisco engaged in organizing residential hotel tenants. Their uncompromising stands on poor people's human rights bolstered the resolve of other housing organizations to address poverty and racism and become more resilient against compromise. Working together with groups such as the Central City SRO Collaborative and Religious Witness with Homeless People, the Agenda was part of successful organizing campaigns that greatly improved the quality of life for residential hotel tenants. In 2001, the Board of Supervisors reformed the visitor policies for SROs (effectively getting rid of Mike Dorn's "four-fuck" rule), and in 2003, hotel operators were finally required to put sprinklers in all of their properties. Since that time, not a single residential hotel has been permanently lost for housing. Sustained organizing from hotel tenants resulted in the repair of all of the scorched hotels and their being turned over to nonprofit social-housing providers.

Beyond the skill and savvy of organizers, how was it that SRO tenants were able to make so many tangible gains? One reason is that the media was far more likely to portray them as the "deserving" poor, in contrast to the mostly negative portrayal of public housing resident. In addition, residential hotel landlords were routinely taken to task for the condition of their properties by the press. Also, at a time when the city was under immense pressure to curb visible homelessness in commercial centers, advocates were able to pose SRO stabilization as a low-cost solution.

If there are lessons to be drawn from this part of San Francisco's history, they are fairly straightforward. Disasters, such as hotel fires are rarely natural phenomenon. Like a hurricane, they exposed the contradictions of a liberal city's relationship to its poorest residents. In San Francisco, it took a push from below to achieve very basic safeguards. Such accomplishments are rarely achieved otherwise.

## On a Mission

I've argued at various points in this book how important it is for neighborhood organizers to simultaneously build independent, disruptive politics while engaging fully with opportunities to forestall displacement in the formal legislative and electoral politics. I won't belabor the point here and instead will explore the role of nonprofit housing developers in the overall politics of displacement.

In *Solidarity Divided: The Crisis in Organized Labor and a New Path toward Social Justice*, Fernando Gapasin and Bill Fletcher explore the power dynamics that made the labor movement narrow and conservative.[2] Much of their framework, aimed at creating social-justice unionism, can be applied to large nonprofit housing developers. Both influence the lives of many hundreds of thousands of ordinary people. Both have progressive potential curtailed by constant cooptation pressures. The growth of contemporary unions can be traced back to the upheavals of the Great Depression and subsequent Red Scare. The trajectory of contemporary nonprofit housing developers is linked to the 1960s call for self-determination in communities of color and the resulting normalization of a part of movement demands. The firings of key progressive and left organizers from Mission Housing Development Corporation reflected the tension between those who preferred a narrowly focused organization and those who wished to see it fully engage with the displacement fights. The first approach embraced much of the economic development going on in the community, and posited that there really was no solution to displacement beyond better job-training and community benefits. The second approach asked the organization to set aside immediate advantages and political access in pursuit of a then poorly defined vision of popular power.

Using Gapasin and Fletcher's framework, it is important to understand what nonprofits are, before talking about what they could be. First is the understanding that like unions, community developers have a set of "real-world politics and practices through both internal and external struggles." They are not political parties or radical organizations. In fact, their dependence on public subsidy and private donations likely prevent a complete return to the politics that birthed them. Again echoing Gapasin and Fletcher, nonprofits can't replace social movements. While it is foolish to believe that a nonprofit housing developer will build a movement, it also isn't strategic to automatically dismiss the lot as automatically part of a nonprofit industrial complex.

For, even as the structure of the economy and the demands of providing social housing can domesticate community development centers (CDCs), they are one of the only parts of the urban economy where working-class people do not have to worry about economically motivated evictions. Therefore CDCs are one of the few areas where these communities form a visible, concentrated potential political bloc. Returning neighborhood control to nonprofits is something that must happen both within and outside of them. The first step is for nonprofits to protect their progressive legacies by upholding the rights of their tenants and workers to organize even if it yields uncomfortable short-term conflicts. Nonprofits must see their mission as contributing to the end of problems like displacement, not just servicing it or doing good work despite these problems—which means finding ways to loan resources and technical expertise to organizations that can more fully confront displacement because of their independent nature.

## Human Rights and Insurgent Citizenship

In response to the global dimensions of displacement, many housing rights organizers are promoting the idea of housing as a basic human right. In 2008, the United States received a visit from United Nations Special Rapporteur, Raquel Rolnik, a Brazilian academic. Rolnik met with housing organizations and government officials to analyze the US housing crisis in Washington, DC, New York, Chicago, New Orleans, San Francisco, Los Angeles, and the Pine Ridge Reservation. Housing as a human right is embedded in the Universal Declaration of Human Rights:

> **Article 25:** Everyone has the right to a standard of living adequate for the health and well-being of himself and of his family, including food, clothing, housing and medical care and necessary social services, and the right to security in the event of unemployment, sickness, disability, widowhood, old age or other lack of livelihood in circumstances beyond his control.

Though recognized as international law in a subsequent International Covenant on Economic, Social and Cultural Rights, the United States has never ratified it. In 2010 Rolnik's own recommendations were useful but stopped far short of questioning the basic pillars of property and land. She recommended more affordable housing, and an end to budget cuts to housing-assistance programs, a moratorium on demolition of public housing, and an end to criminalization of homeless people.[3] Sara Shortt of the Housing Rights Committee of San Francisco believes that the process yielded little short-term results but helped legitimize the demands of domestic housing-rights organizers. "It brought attention to the fact that the US and SF in particular has serious housing problems on par [with] other international housing rights issues, and that we are not exempt from the same human rights violations as what people tend to associate with 'developing nations.'"

Human rights are curious animals, as they are embedded in the constitutions of countries that routinely ignore them. The Constitution of South Africa upholds the human right of housing, though shantytowns pockmark the post-apartheid landscape. The concept of insurgent citizenship advances the ideal that citizenship is not only made by formal constitutions, covenants, and declarations but by the actions of those impacted by poverty and inequality. Sometimes these actions remain autonomous of the state, other times they lead to reforms. They complicate the notion of citizenship by reimagining it as something created from below, not granted from above.[4] Insurgent citizenship is reflected when public-housing residents "vote with their butts" and refuse to move, in eviction blockades, rent strikes, squatting, and street mobilizations. It's an alternative form of ratification of human rights. It's hard to imagine the United States recognizing the right to housing, much less what it might do if it did. Yet it is the action that breathes life into the ideals.

It's easy to be cynical about the human rights approach to housing. It's unlikely that the United Nations is likely to impose sanctions on the United States or dispatch housing peacekeepers to prevent the demolition of public housing. Yet even unenforceable mandates can serve to elevate demands and expectations. A human rights framework cuts through much of the ideological morass of who deserves housing in the global economy. As Rob Robinson, of Take Back the Land, observes, "The framework is based on need versus the ability to pay. Poor people in the US traditionally have not been able to secure housing through the market process for a number of reasons. There is a long history of discrimination against the poor and people of color, and the US has ignored human rights law. The UN Declaration of Human Rights says—we all have rights to which all human beings are inherently entitled. If we are to meet the needs of humans, we need to ensure the availability of housing that meets human needs."[5]

When one loses housing, there seem to be a thousand voices that explain why this is the fault of the displaced. *They shouldn't have had so many kids. They should have saved more money to buy a home of their own. They are illegal. They should have read the fine print in the mortgage document.*

A human rights framework shuts this down. If housing is a right, then it is a right that is to be enjoyed by virtue of being human. In itself this is a counterbalance to a half-century of neoliberal destruction of the commons and centuries of fetishizing private property as the basis of the American Dream. Also, the idea that housing should be guaranteed to all humans shakes the traditional liberal and conservative goalposts of housing policy, both of which operate under the umbrella of private market logic. In practical terms, this means that development that serves the interests of the majority of people will be secondary to that serving the minority. Little affordable housing is built unless a greater amount of luxury housing is first produced—the business-as-usual web of inclusionary housing policies, tax-increment financing, and guarantee this disparity.[6]

## Taking Left and Right Turns to the Local

Today's representational democracy provides little representation or democracy, but plenty of power pushed upward to planners and elites. It's no surprise that so many social movements addressing inequalities in the global economy propose a turn toward the local. Local solutions, such as community land trusts, participatory budgeting, and neighborhood councils play an important role in winning immediate improvements in people's lives, while normalizing cooperation and mutuality. The impulse toward governance that can be seen, heard, and articulated with your neighbors is a worthwhile project, however, it should never be taken for granted that decisions in a better society would automatically be made at the smallest possible unit. Blindly pursuing the local as the cure-all for the sins of the economy ignores the troubled history of the decentralization—especially as it pertains to cities and race. Shifting governance from federal to local control has long been a centerpiece of the racist arguments against basic democratic demands of black citizens.

The turn toward the local can only be effective if it grapples with today's distinct limits of local and neighborhood control. A great portion of the social responsibilities once borne by the federal government (housing, education, amelioration of poverty) has already been foisted on cash-starved cities. Local control already exists in a dystopian form. Behind every school closure and every budget cut are the politics of scarcity and austerity. Absent are the tools to actually achieve long-term solutions or new forms of governance, which has led to pessimism about the long-term impact of urban social movements. If one of the major pillars of the housing crisis is deregulated capital, then what good is your local cooperative? Has globalization made neighborhood politics passé?

Neoliberalism's architect Friedrich Hayek wrote that he preferred the complete removal of the regulatory state, but decentralization was the best way to provide goods and services should private capital be unwilling to take up the task.[7] In the United States, the most vocal proponents of local control have historically not been interested in a cooperative commonwealth, but rather racist segregation and domination masquerading as states' rights.

Local reforms often happen because social movements and the corporate right agree on the same reform for vastly different reasons. Take, for instance, the growth of the nonprofit sector in urban areas. Nonprofits absorbed many of the functions previously held by the state, such as providing social housing. In addition, local governments were clever to depoliticize "Survival Pending Revolution" programs promoted by groups like the Black Panther Party (e.g., food pantries, literacy projects) by absorbing them into liberal municipal regimes. Did this symbolize the transformation of existing institutions so that they finally served the needs of oppressed people?

At the left edge of the spectrum, this implied a world whose basic unit of governance was based in the neighborhood or the workplace, preferably in a post-capitalist or transitional arrangement.[8] Most of the advocates of local control had witnessed the top-down and often dehumanizing impacts of the War on Poverty and the Model Cities Program. For others, local control was an attempt to put teeth on the anti-racist project, advancing from civil rights to economic power.

What was perhaps not fully grappled with was that the political right was just fine with local control on its own terms. Implicit in the assault on social welfare was an exchange: increased municipal control but more austerity. The Western Regional Advocacy Project deftly traced the federal government's retreat from providing social housing and identified how this catalyzed homelessness. Between 1978 and 1983, the budget for the US Department of Housing and Urban Development was slashed by over $65 billion. Since 1996, no new dollars for public housing have been added to the federal budget, though hits to operating reserves have made it impossible for localities to maintain decent living conditions in existing public housing.[9] The task for progressive organizers is to articulate a form of participatory governance in jagged contradiction to the austerity agenda.

### The Return of the City-State?

Cities are assuming more of the functions of the federal government. The grand shell game sells austerity under the wrapper of local autonomy. For the foreseeable future, domestic community organizing will continue to pursue local agendas, even as the ability of local governments to expand the commons will be severely curtailed. Jane Jacobs, in her book *Cities and the Wealth of Nations*, predicted that cities develop as the primary actor in overall economic well-being, supplanting the importance of federal policy. Against these boundaries, urban activists are offered important, if limited, opportunities to build an alternative urbanism.

Globalization also makes cities operate as factories of old once did—where people from all over the globe can meet and find both common ground and conflict. The challenge for organizers is to build the type of local politics that are savvy enough to connect to national and international questions. The Occupy Wall Street movement almost accomplished this by using the city as the launching point for critiques of debt, foreclosures, and enclosures, and it is no surprise that as Occupy receded, the approach of many of its finest veterans was to turn toward their neighbors (Occupy the Hood, Occupy Housing) or begin ambitious workplace organizing campaigns. Cities can be incubators for inclusive new forms of production, social consumption, and development. A program of alternative urbanism should place demands on the state and build popular grassroots power as the San Francisco Community Land Trust and Dudley Street Neighborhood Initiative have attempted to do. It should:

- Reduce the cost of urban living by removing key area of social consumption from the market place.
- Expand and redefine the commons, production, and ownership for public use over private profit.
- Recognize the city, even in its most dystopian form, as having the potential to generate new forms of equity, modes of production, and political participation.
- Create opportunities for people to experiment with new social norms, with mutual aid and social solidarity replacing excessive competition and greed.
- Attempt to build popular power in excluded communities, as opposed to simply building superior ways of providing social resources in a capitalist context.

If we are serious about fighting for municipal commons, several conditions have to be met. In the short term, urban social movements must be sharp enough to navigate existing electoral-legislative arrangements, while maintaining independent politics and a willingness to use direct action. Blanket abstention from the electoral process allows right-wing control of city budgets, rent stabilization, and public health. Paradoxically, movements that are swallowed by electoral politics often deteriorate under its weight.

A special kind of public infrastructure is needed in order to challenge the corporate stranglehold on cities. Local taxes, especially in service-economy cities, rarely bring in enough revenue to pay for competing social needs such as housing, transportation, education, and public safety. This creates a grotesque drama. Perhaps the most undignified is the creation of single-issue advocacy where actors representing different concerns (e.g., parks and affordable housing) compete for funds that are never enough to meet all needs. This chains even the most progressive cities to corporate interests at the neck and at the hips. Through municipal bonds, cities become reliant on their ability to borrow money from banks, which means that, should a city want to get serious about fighting foreclosures by expropriating bank-owned homes, Wall Street can retaliate through capital flight and lawsuits meant to punish errant legislators and their constituents.

Richmond, California, a working-class city across the bay and just north of San Francisco, has started down this road, with real estate interests including Fannie Mae and Freddie Mac leading a corporate legal, political, and public relations offensive against it.[10] Just south, in Oakland, labor unions alleged that Wall Street had robbed the struggling city of about $468 million through manipulation of interests rates.[11] In San Francisco, activists working with Supervisor John Avalos have pursued the idea of a locally owned bank so that public needs can be financed without outside interference and blackmail. Without fortifying the autonomy of cities like this, even the strongest social movement or most progressive populist politician will be stuck scrabbling at the edges of the crisis.

### What can be, What should be.

> Lacking perspectives and positive accomplishments, the revolutionary flame begins to dim. Certainly, capitalism is incapable of fundamentally resolving the essential problems which its development has brought about.
>
> —Andre Gorz, *Strategy for Labor*

If business-as-usual housing is killing our cities, what can activists offer in the way of alternatives? This isn't a new question or debate. Friedrich Engels wrote "The Housing Question" to admonish Pierre-Joseph Proudhon about utopian housing schemes. Proudhon favored mutual aid and cooperative housing, and didn't give much credence to state ownership. Engels got it partially right as housing prices are indeed tied to the capitalist production cycle, but he dismissed the idea of any sort of housing reforms, relegating them to after-the-revolution status. This outlook might have been more useful in the earlier days of industrial capitalism and urbanization. Today it is safe to say that struggles for space and place will unfold alongside, and often in place of, traditional workplace organizing. It is also impossible to build a better world one cooperative at a time. It is possible for housing reforms to contribute to a larger movement and build everyday people's confidence in collective action. Even taken in absence of a larger vision, attempts to survive and regain some dignity in a dehumanizing economy contribute to a stronger social fabric.

We are all too well adjusted to an economic system that evicts, downsizes, pollutes, and imprisons. This same system also comes equipped with a well-oiled public relations system calibrated to rob us of something even more profound: our ability to imagine a different state of affairs. Many are familiar with Margaret Thatcher's TINA (There Is No Alternative) admonition. The idea that human and economic relationships are at the end of their history might seem absurd, but it is widely felt even among casualties of the marketplace. In 1963, French economist and philosopher Andre Gorz set out, in *Strategy for Labor: A Radical Proposal*, to convince revolutionaries to take reform seriously. From the vantage point of the post–World War II social contract, he argued that material deprivation was no longer a sufficient kindle for social movements. Gorz proposed that the battle to overcome alienation and meaninglessness was as important as wages and benefits.

I'm not certain if Gorz ever anticipated that the gains associated with social democracy in Europe (and the New Deal in the United States) would come under such sharp attack—he would have been forced to revise this thesis watching the shredding of income support, union representation, and healthcare guarantees in "advanced" capitalist countries as part of the austerity project. Even if the world economy has changed drastically since 1963, part of his challenge to labor (and the left) is still relevant today. He rallied against the premise that capitalism would "inevitably, catastrophically collapse." Discarding the idea that misery would be the best organizer, he mocked the idea that "working class leaders continue to fear that too great a victory in their everyday struggles will remove—or blunt for a long time—the workers discontent and their revolutionary spirit." The apprehension he described, that partial victory within the capitalist framework would simply reinforce the system, is one that is echoed time and again in contemporary activist discourse.[12] But lacking actual tangible accomplishments, promises of building "another world" seem hollow. Gorz provided insight into the nature of reform fights, arguing that the "struggle for reform is not necessarily reformist," while acknowledging a large grey area between reforms meant to bolster capitalism and those with intent to illustrate the confines of the system while meeting actual needs. To him a reformist will subordinate objectives rooted in human needs to the logic of capitalism. By contrast there is another option: pursuing the types of anti-capitalist reforms not determined by "what can be, but what should be."

Gorz's ideas are similar to what subsequent generations of radicals would call prefigurative politics, the idea of which has assumed an almost sacred place in the aspirations of many corners of the left. But what does it mean to "prefigure" a revolution in the way people live? Webster's dictionary offers one definition: to picture or imagine before hand. In reaction to common top-down models of social-change organizing, prefiguration's enthusiasts attempt to provide a sneak preview of what a better world might look like through their present-day actions.

These insights are particularly relevant for today's radicals, who operate in cities. When those with a long-term egalitarian vision excuse themselves from dealing with conditions of everyday life, there are those who are more than willing to fill the void. It is scarcity that compels a tradesperson to support building multimillion-dollar condominiums they and their families could never afford to live in. When there are alternatives, few people actually invite Walmart and other minimum-wage giants into their neighborhoods.

It's taken a while for prefiguration to step into the center of activist concerns, but the idea is nothing new—it can be traced to the Industrial Workers of the World's slogan "making a new world in the shell of the old," Gandhi's "be the change you want to see in the world," and the radical feminist maxim that "the personal is political." This book is about is possibility of taking prefigurative politics to scale, test-piloting new forms of urban life without derailing the larger project of transformative politics.

It can often be hard for radicals to think through what their own alternative urban agenda would look like. This is understandable as doing so brings us into uncharted waters, but there's no reason why a strategy to take away capital's ability to blackmail us through scarcity can't be countered with a vision—a non-alienated city rebuilt by and for for those whom the neoliberal project has failed the most.

## A Strategy for Cities: An Eviction-Free City?

An effective strategy in the housing crisis will combine immediate emergency tactics such as eviction moratoriums, inside a long-term strategy of building a popular self-managed housing sector. Eviction moratoriums have a historical precedent: in the 1930s, the unemployed workers' movements succeeded in winning moratoriums largely through highly disruptive protest strategies. Cities including Detroit and Toledo, Ohio, embraced moratoriums, which allowed renters to survive the Great Depression. Militant eviction protests and rent strikes across the United States forced cities to enact rent control and build more social housing; in the absence of government intervention, direct action is one of the few tactics that contest speculators' ability to evict and displace.

Strong rent controls and stiff regulatory protections against evictions are essential to fighting displacement, but social contracts can be broken, especially in the face of a well-funded landlord lobby. If the landlords have any valid arguments, it is that it is unrealistic to explect small property owners to be long-term social-housing providers. A housing program that gets to the root of the problems will fight to bring housing out of the speculative market and into the social sphere. Domestic land reform is certainly far off on the political horizon, yet the foundation of an anti-displacement program is remarkably easy to conceive by countering the assumptions of neoliberals with their opposites. Where property speculation is allowed to destroy communities: sabotage speculation. When the commons are privatized: propose new forms of commons that exist beyond the market and the state.

Of all interventions, anti-speculation measures may have the most impact in a wide variety of housing struggles. Organizers in many cities are seeking measures that would tax away profits made by the practice of quickly buying and selling housing for a quick gain, while evicting tenants. Anti-speculation approaches can also be applied to privatization battles, ensuring that private investors in public housing do not receive such windfalls as to incentivize displacement of residents. As of this writing, housing organizers in San Francisco are preparing an anti-speculation measure for the November 2014 ballot. It is an important moment, as it signals a new willingness to challenge the foundations of the displacement crisis. Popular education will be critical, as even victims of evictions can recoil at proposals that seem too strident against private property. It should be assumed that if a measure is won at the ballot box, speculators might seek to undermine it through legal and procedural trickery. Mass mobilization and direct action will be necessary to expand such a strident new front in the war for home.

Cities, acting together as regions, should demand the resources to construct massive amounts of new social housing, enough to eliminate waiting lists and increase supply. As we saw in Chapter 1, public housing was handicapped from the start, as access to it was restricted only to those so poor that even slumlords wouldn't be interested in renting to them, which undercut broad support for public housing. Later, privatizers give lip service shrunk the amount of housing available for poor communities, under reactionary versions of "mixed-income" programs. To counter this, housing organizers should demand not only a halt to the loss of low-income housing, but its increase. New housing, which addresses the needs of people from a variety of income levels—from government-aid recipients to middle-income workers such as teachers and construction workers—can be built. Doing so would subvert both the conservative agenda of shrinking social housing at the expense of poor people, and the liberal tendency to advocate for housing only for those "most in need."[13]

The forty-year disinvestment cycle in public housing is a good example of the neoliberal agenda of running public resources to the ground, so that privatization will be welcomed. Even in cities with strong anti-privatization politics, the shortest route to improving dilapidated buildings will be to break up public housing authorities (PHAs). Another option is available: rebuilding public housing with public funds, while simultaneously cleaning house of the urban administrators who make privatization look like the only alternative. Massive job-creation programs linked to people-led redevelopment of construction and services can provide a pathway out of poverty for many. Echoing the observations of many public-housing organizations, there should be an immediate moratorium on any "plan" involving displacement of residents and the loss of needed units.

Perhaps a starting point for the future of public housing here might be the housing program of Vienna in the 1920s. Local politics in Vienna were largely controlled by the Social Democratic Party, who were committed to the right to housing for the majority of people. Funded through progressive taxation, over 58,000 units of housing in a thirteen-year period were created. The homes of "Red Vienna" were revolutionary in the sense that rents contributed to the upkeep of the buildings, instead of being tied to percentages of what "fair" market rent would look like. Anton Weber, who headed Vienna's housing bureau during this period, described the politics:

> The crowning feature of the social policy of Vienna since 1919 has been the guarantee of shelter for every one and the provision of modern, wholesome dwellings. The city government of Vienna regards the building of homes as the task of the whole community, just as it does the erection of school buildings and hospitals. The present Vienna City Council, in an overwhelming majority, is of the opinion that the unwholesome housing conditions under which the population of Vienna suffers in the present day are due to the fact that the provision of housing down to 1918 was left to private enterprise. A good roomy, well-lighted dwelling is a major cultural factor in the life of every people. A damp, dark dwelling is the nesting place of disease; it sends to the hospitals and tuberculosis sanitariums un-productive human material which burdens the community more than would the building of proper dwellings.

Vienna's experiment with the human right of housing was stopped abruptly in 1934 when fascist forces unleashed a barrage of heavy artillery on the Karl Marx Hof. While it is senseless to romanticize housing programs over nine decades past, Vienna's example shows a sharp contrast to what is considered the left edge of today's public-policy housing debates.[14]

Recently, mayors of both San Francisco and Oakland announced housing initiatives that proposed that the majority of new homes constructed would be unaffordable to most working people.[15] Urban policy in the United States has been trapped in the cage of private market logic. In practical terms, this means that development that serves the interests of the majority of people will be secondary to that serving the minority. It is important for organizers to fight for fundamental changes in how housing is shared, rather than just advocating for more rights in the existing balance of power. Today, little affordable housing is built unless a greater amount of luxury housing is first produced.[16]

## All Things in Common

But what of the existing housing stock? I remember attending a public hearing at San Francisco City Hall where the idea of community land trusts was being discussed. During public comment, a group of elderly women testified that the city would seize their residences and force them into collective ownership. Such an approach would not only be immoral, it would build a determined constituency against radical housing solutions. For those for whom private ownership works, there is no reason to force them into other arrangements for the sake of ideology; bringing more and more housing out of the speculative market and into the social sphere can be accomplished without this. Vacant foreclosed and tax-delinquent homes can be brought into public ownership by seizing the properties from banks and absentee landlords. Such buildings can become part of a community land trust, mutual housing association, or a public-ownership network. Cities should provide land trusts, and other cooperative housing organizations, the finances and the regulatory power to acquire housing in jeopardy of eviction to keep them affordable in perpetuity.

Reconstructing a society-wide commitment to housing will involve public investment. This is unavoidable if alternative urbanism is to grow to scale, beyond scattered good examples and counter-cultural experiments. But more equitable cities can't be achieved through government programs and social services alone. Solely stat-ist strategies deprive communities of the dignity of creating their own futures. Society as a whole loses when the responsibility for creative solutions is relinquished to managers and elected officials. Housing organizing must include what I call the "second demand" beyond those for primary relief: that demand is the project of build-ing effective popular power and grassroots decision making to govern and defend radical reforms. Today, through community planning and participatory budgeting efforts, everyday people are experimenting with what future governance might look like.

In his book *New York for Sale: Community Planning Confronts Global Real Estate*, Tom Angotti maps out another urban fu-ture where the development of cities is shaped by ordinary people through decentralized community-planning methods. According to Angotti, director of Hunter College's Community Planning and De-velopment Department, this future may well exist within the shell of today's economy. As evidence, he points to over seventy communi-ty-driven plans in New York City alone, many of which have sprung from the city's fights against displacement in the past four decades. A comprehensive survey of all such plans would take several volumes, so only two are explored in detail: the 1961 Cooper Square Com-mittee plan and the We Stay–Nos Quedamos plan in the Melrose Commons section of the South Bronx.

In the case of Cooper Square, determined activists moved from protest to planning and forced the city's developers to severely curtail an urban renewal scheme. They succeeded and, through the growth of community development corporations, were able to create new affordable housing and preserve existing stock. In Melrose Com-mons, largely Latino renters and small businesspeople mobilized to confront a developer who would have displaced over seventy-eight homeowners, four hundred tenants, eighty businesses, and five hun-dred workers. Through strategic community organizing, the We Stay group made the city accept a plan based on 168 neighborhood con-sultations.

Angotti's vision of city planning is an ambitious one: he uses the term "progressive community planning" to describe a process that can "achieve local and global equality, social inclusion, and environmental justice." In part, this description is made as an attempt to differentiate the planning Angotti proposes from racist, NIMBY-driven "community plans," which serve to exclude and further dislocate low-income communities.

## Every Cook Can Budget?

One of today's promising non-housing urban experiments is participatory budgeting (PB), a formal process where everyday citizens are given the authority to vote and deliberate over a portion of a municipal budget. City budgets are boring by design; unless you are a city employee or contractor, chances are that you pay attention to anything but your city's budget as it is hammered out in tedious public hearings. Behind the wall of monotony, life and death decisions are made by a dozen or so people who determine whether or not children are educated, emergency calls answered, or if basic health services provided. Budget forensics often provide clues to who in your city is getting the tax breaks, kickbacks and sweetheart deals. Decipher one and you have a virtual road map of exactly who is getting over on whom. Given this, city officials have tremendous incentives to keep as many people away from the process as possible.

PB was formed in 1989 in Porto Alegre, Brazil, by the Workers Party (or Partido Trabahadores) and has always been a study in contradictions. It is a step toward participatory democracy, where citizens must meet face-to-face a decide priorities as a society together. Yet it is highly dependent on traditional representative democracy and relationships with elected officials.

One of the most unlikely places for participatory budgeting to take root is Vallejo, California. Vallejo is a tough town—blue collar, Democratic for the most part, but a far cry from the type of activism that is self-satisfied in its progressivism. Vallejo has its spasms of occasional uprisings and controversies: it briefly hosted a small chapter of the Black Panther Party; in 1989, it was the site of a grand anti-racist mobilization when Nazi skinheads attempted to hold a white power conference there; residents of subsidized housing in the Marina made national headlines for resisting law-enforcement raids based solely on welfare status. More recently, there have been pitched battles around police brutality, and Native Americans have mobilized to reclaim burial grounds slated for paving.

Vallejo is only half an hour north of San Francisco, but it might as well be on the other side of the continent. San Francisco's love affair with all things that Tweet and Yammer (and the accompanying tidal wave of wealth and development) are irrelevant here. Vallejo never fully recovered from the closure of its navy base in 1996. In an all too familiar story, the city didn't have a good enough plan for life after the navy, where rumors of peace dividends ended up to be simply that: rumors. An army of service sector jobs couldn't replace the loss of the high-paying work that sustained the distribution jobs, small businesses, and the tax base. With the loss of a key industry, Vallejo was especially exposed during the financial meltdown. In 2008, the city went bankrupt. Expenses like decent pensions for municipal workers, once easier to finance, were blamed in a one-note fashion for murdering the city budget. Yet even if the firefighters had been more willing to part with their pensions, the crisis would have been merely forestalled. A city can't survive as it's losing to foreclosures what's left of its tax base.

Today, Vallejo's books are officially balanced, but the scars are still evident. Vallejoans have gotten used to fewer city services, shuttered schools. Prosperity, once a hallmark of the suburbs, has moved away. Vallejo also copes with a massive violent crime problem: as the city escaped bankruptcy in 2012, it did so during one of the largest spikes in the murder rate in twenty-five years. It might seem strange then, that a city like Vallejo would dabble in participatory budgeting. It's financial house is barely in order, and already it plunges in to a grand experiment, the first citywide PB initiative in the United States.

Vallejo is more than a collection of problems. It is also a study in resiliency. Ask people here what they like about Vallejo, and they talk sincerely about neighbors and neighborhoods, their churches and schools. There are stories about knowing Vallejo's famous sons and daughters like musicians E-40 and Con Funk Shun "back in the day." Vallejoans have a sense of self-reliance and volunteerism. One woman shared with me how she and her neighbors banded together to clean their streets when budget cuts decimated debris collection. Another volunteered to keep her kid's school library open. In

Vallejo's PB process, any resident of Vallejo who is sixteen years of age or older may vote. The Steering Committee consciously included immigrant residents, regardless of legal status. At the Vallejo Adult School, I asked about a dozen people if this was a concern to them at all. In this very unscientific exit poll, not a whiff of controversy was detected. Reactions ranged from "Sure, why not?" to "They pay taxes and send their kids to the same schools we do." Also absent was high-minded political rhetoric. Including your neighbors is simply a neighborly thing to do.

Another strength is that PB breaks down the idea that the suffrage project is over and confined to representative democracy. Not a US citizen? Not a problem—you can still participate. Does a pockmarked criminal record keep you from voting? participatory budgeting still welcomes you. Not legally an adult? That's fine, because most cities include high school students. PB's main problem is whether it will be absorbed into the overall austerity agenda, or if it will become a tool to combat it. So far, the project has stayed far away from questions of progressive taxation or fighting budget cuts. If it continues this way, it will be a fatal flaw. What use is it to participate in an ever-shrinking budget? It's comparable to placing a full meal on the table, but telling a guest that she can only eat the potatoes.

Vallejo wasn't the first city in the United States to adopt participatory budgeting: Chicago did so in 2009, when Alderman Joe Moore opted to let the people decide how to spend "his" $1 million in discretionary city funding. Like most cities in the United States, the mayor's office generates the budget and dominates the process. Aldermen and alderwoman can tinker around the edges if they don't step too far out of line. The consolation prize is discretionary funds.

A million dollars doesn't go very far in the city, but it's enough to build patronage and political favors. It's just a small enough amount that in a city filled with needs, an alderman or alderwoman will have to make choices, and eventually alienate somebody. Rachel Weber, an assistant professor of urban planning at the University of Illinois at Chicago sees connections between old Chicago and new. "Chicago-style machine politics meant that you had a boss who commands the support of a corps of campaign workers who participate by getting out the vote for the party boss on Election Day. And then they receive rewards for their loyalty: patronage jobs, public investment in their neighborhoods, and building permits." The consternation in Chicago is emblematic of the challenges ahead if this experiment is to grow in scale. At this point in history, its necessary for PB's promoters to work with elected officials. Often these officials are invested in the project but also unwilling to do the heavy lifting to make the process expansively inclusive. Worse, they can also be the same people who are generally fine with how the global economy shapes the city, down to the last closed school house. Alderman Moore was widely criticized for the hypocrisy of promoting PB while embracing Mayor Rauhm Emmanuel's school closures and his move to replace an elected school board with an appointed one.

At some point PB's partisans will be faced with some hard choices. PB can evolve to mobilize a large base of people to demand new forms of urban social justice, or it can become window dressing for austerity. The project has a lot of positive aspects to build from: it engages everyday people and builds a basis of social solidarity; it can, under the right circumstances expose, rather than obscure, the political economy of cities.

### Gathering Forces to Win

Urban movements must move beyond the "politics of no" and aggressively define what kinds of development they wish to see. This approach is beyond rhetorical value. Corporate developers are almost always able to drive a wedge between potential allies if they promise jobs, while deriding opponents of displacing projects as anti-development ideologues who care nothing for blue-collar construction workers. Simply opposing development, while often necessary, practically builds an army of opposition in trade unions, unemployed people, and communities of color. This means a shift in the organizing strategies for many accustomed to protesting the latest luxury condominium development or big-box store.

Setting an alternative-development agenda can be daunting, especially if local activists view all development with suspicion. The example of the Evergreen Cooperatives in Cleveland, Ohio, is a strong example of economic development that is not chained to corporate logic. They operate a industrial laundry service, solar energy installation firm, and a greenhouse under a cooperative, employee-owned framework. Rooted in communities of color, the presence of opportunities such as this will diminish the ability of corporate developers to push displacing development under the mantra of jobs. Many campaigns to increase the security of workers, such as living wage and fast food organizing, can have similar impacts. However, it is examples like Evergreen that suggest a path away from a casual precarious economy toward a dignified one.

Displacement is a phenomenon that eventually harms the entire working class of a city and eventually reaches far beyond it to artistic communities and certain rungs of the middle class. The vast majority of solutions should advance housing as a human right. However, where communities of color have been particularly targeted by removal by government and corporations, it is reasonable to demand reparations for the dispossession. In a capitalist society, stable versions of home ownership accrue to the owner a host of advantages that can translate into economic survival for their children and even grandchildren. The urban renewal programs that shrunk land ownership in black and brown communities had ripple effects on college entrances, healthcare outcomes, and life expectancy. Reparations could be easily monetized or paid in the form of land grants to descendants of urban renewal victims.

## Another City Is Possible?

Housing organizers are often fond of saying that "another city is possible," adapting a well-worn slogan from the global-justice movement. Making it possible is not only a matter of having good ideas but building power capable of uprooting the exclusion so hard-wired into the economies of today's cities. Since the way we organize is largely shaped by local conditions and politics, I've purposely remained neutral on the question of what kinds of organizations are best suited to the fight for an inclusive urbanism.

Just like an environmental eco-system, a housing movement needs multiple forms of life to survive. Even the most ethical non-profit housing developer can't produce enough social housing to stem displacement. All of them come up against the tall walls of the funders' demands and regulations. On the other end of the spectrum, many of the scrappy direct-action organizations will come and go overtime. Activists should resist the temptation to fetishize one organizational form as the only one capable of contributing to a housing movement.

That said, there are some characteristics that should anchor all organizing in the city. All organizations should reckon with the confines that capitalism places on their best aspirations. Accountability to a participatory democratic practices and self-management to the greatest extent possible may be the best guarantees that a movement will be able to "keep it real." Most importantly, housing movements must demand that which would do the most good for the greatest number of people and not start out with the politics of pragmatism. Any experienced organizer will tell you that a successful campaign will offer plenty of challenging times to consider what kinds of compromises might be necessary. That shouldn't distract us from the fact that being unreasonable in the face of displacement is actually a virtue.

A quick glance at history shows that the fiercest fights for home occur when there are major conversations about society's very foundations. The tenant movement of the 1930s, which achieved lasting reforms, happened against a backdrop of fierce labor organizing and when the legitimacy of capitalism was openly contested. The anti-urban renewal fights of the 1960s and '70s were local expressions of the anti-imperialist and Third World movements—even if that was not understood by all of its participants at the time. Social movements and labor upsurges achieve something far beyond their stated goals: they create a new common sense about what human beings deserve both by virtue of being human and in return for their labors. Without this change, all others will be fleeting.

## Acknowledgments and Gratitude

When putting forward any sort of thanks list, one runs the risk of critical omissions. That said, there are more than a few people without whom this book would not have been possible. Thanks to Juliette Torrez, Fernando Marti, Bethola Harper, Benita Grayson, Willie Baptist, Chana Morgenstern, Antonio Diaz, Amie Fishman, Chris Selig, Holly Krig, Jacoba Cruz, Oscar Grande, Paul Boden, Laura Guzman, Nato Green, Bucky Sinister, Joe Wilson, Lisa Cleis, Amy Sonnie, Ben Shepard, Lynn Lewis, Brandon King, Sam Miller, Rob Robinson, Tom Wetzel and Wendy Kramer of the San Francisco Public Library, and many others. Thanks to my eagle-eyed editors Zach Blue and Lorna Vetters for whipping the manuscript into shape and Kate Khatib for a beautiful cover. If I owe you thanks and left you off the list, drinks are on me.

# Recommended Reading:

## Books

Tom Angotti, *New York for Sale: Community Planning Confronts Global Real Estate*, MIT Press, 2008.
> Excellent overview of community planning models in New York City.

Willie Baptist and Jan Rehmann, *Pedagogy of the Poor: Building the Movement to End Poverty*, Teachers College Press, 2011.
> Baptist's four decades of anti-poverty organzing inform this important book.

Karl Beitel, *Local Protest, Global Movements: Capital, Community and State in San Francisco*, Temple University Press, 2013.
> Explains the political economy of San Francisco and key electoral fights for the right to the city.

Rachel G. Bratt, Michael E. Stone, Chester Hartman: *A Right to Housing: Foundation for a New Social Agenda*, Temple University Press, 2006.
> Pragmatic yet visionary essays on the path to establishing the right to housing in the United States.

Jaron Browne, Marisa Franco, Jason Negron Gonzales, *Towards Land, Work & Power: Charting a Path of Resistance to US Led Imperialism*, Unite-to-Fight Press, 2006.
> Theory drawn from the organizing work of People Organized Winning Employment Rights.

Chris Carlsson, *Reclaiming San Francisco: History, Politics, Culture*, City Lights Books, 1998.
> Collection of essays on the hidden histories of San Francisco.

Anders Corr, *No Tresspassing: Squatting, Rent Strikes, and Land Struggles Worldwide*, South End Press, 1999.
> Great pieces on squatting and direct action, with a lot of background information about Homes Not Jails, SF.

Hanna Dobbz, *Nine-Tenths of the Law: Property and Resistance in the United States*, AK Press, 2012.
> Serious discussion of squatting and anti-authoritarian approaches to housing.

Lisa Gray-Garcia, aka Tiny, *Criminal of Poverty: Growing Up Homeless in America*, City Lights Books, 2006.
> Personal memoir from the co-founder of *Poor Magazine*.

Estella Habal, *San Francisco's International Hotel: Mobilizing the Filipino American Community in the Anti-Eviction Movement*, Temple University Press, 2008.
> The key text about the pivotal struggle to save the International Hotel.

Chester Hartman, *City for Sale: The Transformation of San Francisco*, University of California Press, 2002 and *Yerba Buena: Land Grab and Community Resistance in San Francisco*, National Housing and Economic Development Law Project, 1974.
> Seminal texts of 1960s and '70s displacement in San Francisco.

David Harvey, *Rebel Cities: From the Right to the City to the Urban Revolution*, Verso Books, 2012.
> Unorthodox Marxist exploration of cities and their social movements.

Matt Hern, *Common Ground in a Liquid City: Essays in Defense of an Urban Future*, AK Press, 2010.
> Beautifully written essays about cities and community.

Amy Howard, *More Than Shelter: Activism and Community in San Francisco Public Housing*, University of Minnesota Press, 2014.
Groundbreaking work on public housing, emphasizing activism and agency of residents.

Andy Merrifield, *Dialectical Urbanism: Social Struggles in the Capitalist City*, Monthly Review Press, 2002.
Radical political economy with refreshing attention to the lives of people, especially SRO residents, impacted by displacement.

Mike Miller, *A Community Organizers Tale: People and Power in San Francisco*, Heyday Books, 2009.
Memoir from one of the most principled and dedicated adherents to the Alinksy model of organizing. Details organizing in the Mission District in the 1960s and '70s.

Max Rameau, *Take Back the Land: Land Gentrification and the Umoja Village Shantytown*, 2nd ed., AK Press, 2013.
Rameau's work not only emphasizes the need for direct action, but black self-determination as well.

Saskia Sassen, *The Global City: New York, London, Tokyo*, Princeton University Press, 1991.
Required reading for those curious about urban economics and finance.

Rebecca Solnit, *Hollow City: The Siege of San Francisco and the Crisis of American Urbanism*, Verso Press 2002.
Solnit explores the loss of culture thanks to displacement in this beautifully written book.

Films

Curtis Choy, *The Fall of the I-Hotel*, Moonchonk Priductions, 1983.

Kevin Epps, *Straight Outta Hunter's Point*, Mastamind Productions, 2001.

Francine Cavanaugh, A. Mark Liiv, Adams Wood, Jeff Taylor, *Boom! The Sound of Eviction*, 2001.

Peter Kinoy, *Takeover: Heroes of the New American Depression*, Skylight Films, 1989.

# Endnotes

## Introduction: Of Delivery Trucks & Landlord Pickets

1   Mark Naison, *Communists in Harlem During the Great Depression* (Chicago: University of Illinois Press, 1983) and Frederick Engels, *The Housing Question,* http://www.marxists.org/archive/marx/works/1872/housing-question/.

2   Rick Butler, *The Fillmore—Neighborhoods: The Hidden Cities of San Francisco* (KQED, 2009).

3   The term "sharing economy" refers to the practice of consumers buying access to goods and services, instead of actually possessing them, such as car shares and musical databases.

4   United Nations Population Fund, *State of World Population Report 2007,* http://www.unfpa.org/public/publications/pid/408.

5   Henri Lefebvre, *The Urban Revolution* (Minneapolis: University of Minneapolis Press, 2003).

6   Right to the City Alliance, www.righttothecity.org.

7   National Low Income Housing Coalition, www.nlihc.org.

8   Michael Reich, Ken Jacobs, and Miranda Dietz, eds., *When Mandates Work: Raising Labor Standards at the Local Level* (Berkeley: University of California Press, 2014).

9   Jed Kolko and David Neumark, "Do California's Enterprise Zones Create Jobs?" Public Policy Institute of California, http://www.ppic.org/content/pubs/report/R_609JKR.pdf

10  James Williams, "Alinsky Discovered Organizing (Like Columbus Discovered America)," *Third Force,* July/August 1996.

11  I rather broadly define "direct action" as "any political tactic operating outside of the dominant formal electoral-legislative decision-making structures in a given society."

12  Tom Knoche, "Organizing Communities," *Social Anarchism* 18 (1993): 21.

13  Saul Alinsky, *Rules for Radicals: A Pragmatic Primer for Realistic Radicals* (New York: Vintage Books, 1989) and *Reville For Radicals* (New York: Vintage Books, 1989).

14  Michael Patrick Leahy, *Rules for Conservative Radicals: Lessons from Saul Alinsky, the Tea Party Movement, and the Apostle Paul in the Age of*

*Collaborative Technologies* (New York: C-Rad Books, 2009).

15 "Playboy Interview: Saul Alinksy: A Candid Conversation," *Playboy* 19, no. 3 (March 1972).

16 Upton Sinclair, *The Jungle* (New York: Bantam Books, 1981).

17 Nicholas Von Huffman, *Radical: A Portrait of Saul Alinsky* (New York: Nation Books, 2010).

18 Robert Fisher, *Let the People Decide: Neighborhood Organizing in America* (New York: Twayne Publishers, 1994).

19 Max Elbaum, *Revolution in the Air: Sixties Radicals Turn to Lenin, Mao and Che* (New York: Verso, 2002).

20 There were notable exceptions. Several organizations of our generation were indeed firm in their outlook: the anarchist Love and Rage Federation and the communist Standing Together Organizing a Revolutionary Movement for example. Both of these small and disciplined organizations played influential roles in shaping the priorities of young people radicalized during the late 1980s and early 1990s—even those who never became members.

21 Renny Golden and Michael McConnell, *Sanctuary: The New Underground Railroad* (New York: Maryknoll Press, 1986).

22 Unfortunately, ACT-UP San Francisco eventually adopted the position that AIDS didn't actually exist. Not surprisingly, most of the members of the denial faction have now passed.

23 Jo Freeman, "The Tyranny of Structurelessness," pamphlet originally published in 1971, www.jofreeman.com.

24 Gloria Munoz-Ramirez, *The Fire and the Word: A History of the Zapatista Movement* (San Francisco: City Lights, 2008).

## Chapter One: Landgrabs & Lies: Public Housing at the Crossroads

1 Public housing authorities are typically chartered under state jurisdiction, created by local cities or counties, and governed primarily by federal law for the purpose of providing housing to very-low-income people.

2 This chapter updates and expands on two articles I wrote on privatization and resistance in public housing in the early 2000s: (with Allison Lum) "Landgrabs, Lies and Levellers," *Street Spirit* 7, no. 6 (June 2001); and "A World of Possibility at 45 Westpoint: Homeless Families and their Friends Provide a Glimpse of What a Really Good Left Could Look Like," *Processed World*, Winter 2004/2005. Thanks to editors Terry Messman and Chris Carlsson.

3    Family Rights and Dignity was a work group of the Coalition on Homelessness, SF, which focussed on the needs of homeless families.

4    Public housing authorities (PHAs) were created when Congress authorized the national Housing Act of 1937.

5    Susan Popkin, "A Decade of HOPE VI: Findings Research and Policy Challenges," Urban Institute, 2004, http://www.urban.org/publications/411002.html.

6    Patrick Hogue, "Housing Bribery Detailed: I Sold Section 8," *San Francisco Chronicle*, August 30, 2000.

7    FIST was organized by Standing Together Organizing a Revolutionary Movement, a Bay-Area-based socialist organization. The organizing at Hayes Valley proved difficult to sustain. "Hoax VI: Dividing Communities, Self Destruction for Public Housing," pamphlet from the personal collection of Steve Williams.

8    The Eviction Defense Network was often ably assisted by other radical organizations such as Fire by Night Organizing Committee, Worker's Voice, and League of Revolutionaries for a New America. The Chinatown Community Development Center played a central and positive role in educating Cantonese- and Mandarin-speaking residents about the HOPE VI process.

9    The gigantic Geneva Towers weren't technically public housing but had come under administration of HUD after many decades of neglect and mismanagement. For background: Mike Miller, Tony Fazio, Spence Limbocker, and Karen Thomas, *The People Fight Back: Building a Tenant Union* (San Francisco: Organizing Training Center, 1979).

10   Nina Siegel, "Flagrant Violation: Hayes Residents Never Agreed to Demolition," *San Francisco Bay Guardian*, March 1996.

11   Orissa Orend, "Showdown in Desire: People, Panthers, Piety, and Police" (New Orleans, self-published pamphlet, 2003).

12   Adam Hellegers, "Reforming HUD's One Strike Public Housing Evictions through Tenant Participation," *Journal of Law and Criminology* 1, no. 90 (1999).

13   One of the longest-running anti-poverty organizations in the United States is the Coalition on Homelessness, San Francisco, www.cohsf.org.

14   Cop watching is the activist tactic of filming interactions between police and civilians so as to discourage acts of police brutality. Selena and Katrina, "Copwatch," *Race Traitor* no. 6 (1996).

15   In January 2001, the Ninth Circuit Court of Appeals eliminated the "one strike" provision, which allowed the evictions of those who were both innocent and ignorant of the crime for which they were being

evicted. Angela Rowen, "Project Tenant Evicted for Son's Crimes," *San Francisco Bay Guardian*, 1999.

16  Inspired by this modest victory, the tenant activists of North Beach drafted a Public Housing Tenant Protection Act (PHTPA) as a city-wide ordinance. Although supported by San Francisco Board of Supervisors president Tom Ammiano, and passed by the Finance and Labor Committee, the measure was eventually killed by Supervisor Amos Brown, who later went on to head the San Francisco branch of the National Association for the Advancement of Colored People. Brown publicly decried the PHTPA as a duplicitous measure designed by white activists (the EDN) to keep black people in slum conditions. In reality, it was designed largely by residents of North Beach Public Housing. Amy L. Howard, *More Than Shelter: Activism and Community in San Francisco Public Housing*, (Minneapolis: University of Minnesota Press, 2014).

17  Founded in 1992, Homes Not Jails is an activist group dedicated to advocating for the use of vacant buildings as homes for low-income people: http://www.sftu.org/hnj.

18  Ballot initiatives to "deal" with homelessness have become a permanent aspect of San Francisco's politics: panhandling (Proposition X, 1992), fingerprinting homeless people for shelters (Proposition V, 1993), slashing county aid (Proposition N, aka Care Not Cash 2002), and aggressive panhandling (Proposition M, 2003), for example.

19  Paul Boden, in conversation with James Tracy, March 2014.

20  For a decade, 1990–2000, California's ballots were filled with major right-wing initiatives supporting new prison construction (Proposition 120, 1991), banning undocumented people from schools and services (Proposition 187, 1994), expanding the prison population (Proposition 184, 1994), the end of affirmative action (Proposition 209, 1996), and the criminalization of youth (Proposition 21). The policy impacts were augmented by relentless media campaigns that characterized youth of color as dangerous and disposed to crime.

21  Yolanda Ward, "Spatial Deconcentration," http://www.abcnorio.org/about/history/spatial_d.html.

22  These numbers are approximate as the EDC only started tracking the whereabouts of evicted *clients* (not every evicted tenant is an EDC client) in 2012. However, it is a pretty reliable snapshot of what happens during times of displacement. Eviction Defense Collaborative. "2012 Eviction Report," http://www.evictiondefense.org/EDC_report_6_smaller.pdf.

23  The Kerner Commission Report, released in 1968, recommended traditional liberal solutions to poverty, such as strengthening the social safety net and increasing job opportunities for inner-city citizens. It also suggested spatial deconcentration as a viable strategy to deter urban uprisings. Inner-city riots were frequent in the 1960s, and San Francisco's largest was in 1966—a community response to the police killing of Matthew Johnson, a sixteen-year-old African-American youth from the Bayview. National Advisory Commission on Civil Disorders, commonly known as the Kerner Commission, was set up to investigate the origins of 160 disorders in 128 cities in the first nine months of 1967.

24  Charlie Goodyear, "Welfare Recipients Awarded Damages; Raid Made Target of Poor in Vallejo," *San Francisco Chronicle*, August 12, 1998. The Eviction Defense Network, Young Comrades, and Bay Area Legal Aid helped residents respond to this high-profile raid, organizing speak-outs and collecting testimony for what would eventually become a successful lawsuit filed by the American Civil Liberties Union.

25  Ralph de Costa Nunez, "Homelessness: It's about Race, Not Just Poverty," City Limits, March 5, 2012, http://www.citylimits.org/conversations/159/homeless-the-role-of-race

26  Melissa Chinchilla, "Social Cohesion and Community Safety in New and Redeveloped Mixed Income Housing," written on behalf of San Francisco Department of Public Health's Program on Health Equity and Sustainability, 2010, https://www.sfdph.org/dph/files/EHSdocs/HDMT/WhitePaperSocial.Cohesion.pdf

27  "Police, Protesters in New Orleans Clash over Public Housing Demolition," CBC News, December 20, 2007.

28  Conversation between Sam Ruiz and the author, February 2014. Ruiz is the executive director of Mission Housing and Development Corporation (MHDC), which operates Valencia Gardens, redeveloped under HOPE VI.

29  Figures from "HOPE VI Units and Bedrooms," memo prepared for the San Francisco Board of Supervisors by the San Francisco Housing Authority (August, 19, 1999). The Housing Authority claimed that the loss of units in two-thirds of the developments, as well as the increase in units elsewhere, was simply due to zoning controls, rather than political pressure. Some developments where homes were lost had an increase in bedrooms, which did little to stem the overall displacement of families.

Chapter Two: Slow Burn: San Francisco's Hotel Residents Walk through the Fire

1. Victor Miller, "Fire Fails to Stop Tenant Rebellion: Former Thor Hotel Residents Organize to Fight Homelessness," *New Mission News*, February 1999. The *New Mission News* was one of the finest examples of independent, neighborhood-based journalism until Miller's death in 2002. He and the paper he led are greatly missed.

2   "Musical rooms" is the street terminology for the practice of evicting residential hotel tenants before the minimum number of days needed to gain eviction protections under the Rent Arbitration and Stabilization Ordinance.

3   Beverly Bramlett and Chris Daly, "Hotels and Promises Go Up in Smoke: San Francisco Tenants Get Fired Up and Confront City Hall," *Street Spirit*, March 1999.

4   Miller, "Fire Fails to Stop Tenant Rebellion." GA=General Assistance, SSI=Social Security Insurance, Workfare=work performed in exchange for welfare.

5   At the time, the Mission SRO Collaborative was a coalition of several groups that teamed up to help stabilize the lives of residential hotel tenants. Today, it is the community-organizing wing of Dolores Street Community Services, active in the of the Mission District since 1982.

6   For more on this approach, see Ontario Coalition Against Poverty's Direct Action Casework Manual, http://ocap.ca/files/caseworkmanual.pdf. This approach is an important update of the "Survival Pending Revolution" model popularized by the Black Panther Party and adopted by other organizations such as the Young Lords Organization and the Young Patriots Organization. They created breakfast, literacy, and health programs that immediately made a difference and agitated for a shift in power. Local governments realized the power of revolutionary community organizations building up neighborhood self-reliance and political analysis through this tactic, and in response, large city-funded food banks, health clinics, and after-school programs were established.

7   For further explorations of the unemployed workers' movements, read Frances Fox Piven and Richard A. Cloward, *Poor People's Movements: Why They Succeed and How They Fail* (New York: Vintage Books, 1979).

8   For a critique of the Piven/Cloward approach to mobilizing over organizing, see Willie Baptist, *Pedagogy of the Poor: Building a Movement to End Poverty* (New York: Teacher's University Press, 2011).

9    Chester Hartman, *Yerba Buena: Land Grab and Community Resistance in San Francisco* (San Francisco: Glide Publications, 1974).

10   Curtis Choy, writer and director, *The Fall of the I-Hotel* (Chonk Moonhunter Productions, 1983).

11   Rod Janzen, *The Rise and Fall of Synanon: A California Utopia* (New York: Nation Books, 2001).

12   Joe Wilson in conversation with the author, May 2014.

## Chapter Three: They Plan for Profits, We Plan for People: Local Politics and International Conversations in the Mission District

1    Galería de la Raza, founded in 1970, is a nonprofit community-based arts organization whose mission is to foster public awareness of, and appreciation for, Chicano/Latino art. http://www.galeriadelaraza .org.

2    René Yañez in conversation with Patrick Piazza, on Pirate Cat Radio, March 2014.

3    Rebecca Solnit, "Google Invades," *London Review of Books* 35, no. 3 (February 2013).

4    Billy Gallagher, "Bay Area's Tech Wages Are Nation's Highest, but Should Entrepreneurs Look Elsewhere as Costs Rise?" *Tech Crunch*, July 20, 2013.

5    Anti-Eviction Mapping Project, http://www.antievictionmappingproject .net.

6    The Gross Domestic Product is the total amount of economic production in a country. http://data.worldbank.org/indicator/NY.GDP.MKTP.CD

7    William Pfaff, "France's Army of the Excluded," *Baltimore Sun*, April 20, 1995.

8    It is almost impossible to estimate how many total households were displaced during this time. Landlord harassment, buyouts, and voluntary moves before official eviction notices drive up the sum considerably. Also not reflected in the official tally are households that simply moved out of San Francisco in order to find a more affordable city to live in. Some have estimated the total 1990s displacement tally at about 100,000 households. While this is an intelligent guess (about 12.5 percent of the total population and around 40 percent of the working-class population), it is still only an estimate.

9    This chapter expands on themes from "A Decade of Displacement," a chapter I wrote for Chris Carlsson, ed., *The Political Edge* (San Francisco: City Lights Books, 2005).

10   The original Nestor Makhno was a Ukrainian anarchist who led an

independent army of peasants during the Bolshevik revolution. He later tried to establish the Ukraine as an anarchist society. Alexandre Skirda, *Nestor Makhno, Anarchy's Cossack: The Struggle for Free Soviets in the Ukraine* (Oakland: AK Press, 2004).

11  Kevin Keating, "See the Breaking Glass, Underneath the Overpass: A Critique of the Mission Yuppie Eradication Project." http//:www. anarchistnews.org.

12  Drawing from the theories of thinkers such as Thomas, Marquard, Salvi, Cassanova, and others, "internal colonialism" refers to hyper-exploitive and unequal relationships to people within the same state. MAC applied this formula to people within the same city.

13  Juana Garcia Cornejo, "Changes in the Horizon: High Tech Companies Move to the Mission," *El Mensajero*, May 17, 2000.

14  Antonio Diaz in conversation with author.

15  Fernando Marti, et al., "Planning against Displacement: A Decade of Progressive Community-Based Planning in the Mission District." *Diálogous: Placemaking in Latino Communities* (New York: Routledge, 2012).

16  An accountability session—a tactic popularized by the Midwest Academy—is a public event where community members give testimony to public officials who are pressed to take yes-or-no positions on community demands. Kim Bobo, et al., *Organizing for Social Change: A Manual for Activists in the 1990s* (Washington, DC: Seven Locks, 1991).

17  Caption under photo, author unknown, *El Reportero/The Reporter*, June 21–July 14, 2000.

18  Edith Alderete, "Mission Dot-Com Pressure Boils Over: Residents, Businesses Demand Changes in Planning Process," *The Independent*, November 4, 2000.

19  Victor Miller, "City Hall Rally against Displacement," *New Mission News*, August 2000.

20  Antonio Diaz, "Race and Space: Dot-Colonization and Dislocation in La Mision," *Shades of Power*, Summer 2000.

21  Ryan Kim, "15 Arrested in Mission Sit-in, Protesters Demand That Dot-Com Find Space for Non-profits Forced from Building," *San Francisco Examiner*, September 22, 2000.

22  Saint Peter's Housing Committee was San Francisco's only Spanish-speaking tenant-advocacy group. In 2010, it merged with Oakland's Causa Justa to form Causa Justa/Just Cause, a Bay-Area-wide tenants organization.

23  Cassi Feldman, "Defending the Barrio: Will Working-Class

Activists Save the Mission?," *San Francisco Bay Guardian*, October 18, 2000.

24 Rosemary Cambra, "The Muwekma Ohlone Tribe of the San Francisco Bay Area," http://www.islaiscreek.org/ohlonehistcultfedrecog.html.

25 Fernando Marti, "The Mission District: A History of Resistance," paper prepared for the Mission Anti-Displacement Coalition, 2006.

26 Mike Miller, *A Community Organizer's Tale: People and Power in San Francisco* (Berkeley: Heyday Books, 2009). This is an essential book for anyone who wants to understand organizing in the Mission in the 1960s and 1970s. Miller represents the very best of Alinsky-inspired organizing.

27 Jason M. Ferreira, "With the Soul of a Human Rainbow: Los Siete, Black Panthers, and Third Worldism in San Francisco," in *Ten Years That Shook The City*, ed. Chris Carlsson (San Francisco: City Lights Books, 2011) and Marjorie Heins, *Strictly Ghetto Property: The Story of Los Siete de la Raza* (San Francisco: Ramparts Press, 1972).

28 Created in 1966, the Model Cities Program was an umbrella for many of the initiatives associated with President Johnson's War on Poverty. While establishing some necessary resources for poor people, the MCP was also known for bureaucratic red tape, being patronizing, intrusive social-service delivery, and political patronage.

29 Amie Fishman, "Community Development Corporations Against Gentrification and Displacement: Leading Community Movements in Park Slope, Brooklyn, and the Mission District of San Francisco" (master's thesis, Robert F. Wagner School of Public Service, New York University, 2006).

30 San Francisco City Charter allows the mayor to fill any supervisor seat that becomes vacant before an election. Mayor Brown excelled at finding elected supervisors plum positions elsewhere so that he could consolidate his power with loyalists.

31 Fishman, "Community Development Corporations Against Gentrification and Displacement."

32 Karl Beitel, *Local Protests, Global Movements: Capital, Community and State in San Francisco* (Philadelphia: Temple University Press, 2013).

33 Cassi Feldman, "Why Can't You Buy This House?," *San Francisco Bay Guardian* 35, no. 44 (August 1–7, 2001).

34 Andrew Beattie, "Market Crashes: The Dotcom Crash," Investopedia, http://www.investopedia.com/features/crashes/crashes8.asp.

Chapter Four: A Shift toward Stewardship: Is the Displacement War Over, If We Want It to Be?

1    John Emmeus Davis, "Origins and Evolution of the Community Land Trust in the United States," in *Community Land Trust Reader*, ed. John Emmeus Davis (Cambridge: Lincoln Institute of Land Policy, 2010).

2    "Highest and best use" is real estate industry jargon that basically posits that the best use of a piece of land is the one that yields the greatest financial use, regardless of all other considerations.

3    Neil Smith, *The New Urban Frontier: Gentrification and the Revanchist City* (New York: Routledge, 1996).

4    Picture the Homeless, *Banking on Vacancy: Homelessness and Real Estate Speculation*, Report published 2012, http://picturethehome-less.org/files/pdf/Banking_on_Vacancy_-_Homelessness_and_Real _Estate_Speculation.pdf.

5    New York has a long tradition of long-term housing occupations and squat defense. A good starting point to learn more is Hannah Dob-bz's *Nine-Tenths of the Law: Property and Resistance in the United States* (Oakland: AK Press, 2012).

6    See Henry George, *Progress and Poverty* (New York: Cosimo Press, 2005) and Ebenezer Howard, *Garden Cities of Tomorrow* (Partnoster Square: Swan Sonnenschein, 1902). Also Davis, "Origins and Evolution of the Community Land Trust in the United States," 6–9.

7    Michal Goldman, writer and director, *At Home in Utopia* (Independent Lens, 2008).

8    Interview with Charles Sherrod by John Emmeus Davis in Davis, ed., *The Community Land Trust Reader* (Cambridge: Lincoln Institute of Land Policy, 2010).

9    "Foreclosure Statistics," Neighbor Works America, http://www.fdic. gov/about/comein/files/foreclosure_statistics.pdf

10   Peter Marcuse's blog was a helpful resource while thinking through the different kinds of CLTs: http://pmarcuse.wordpress.com.

Epilogue: toward an Alternative Urbanism

1    For an excellent and succinct description of how toxic mortgages were aggressively marketed to black communities, see Laura Gottesdiener, *A Dream Foreclosed: Black America and the Fight for a Place to Call Home* (New Jersey: Zuccotti Park Press, 2013).

2    Fernando Gapasin and Bill Fletcher, *Solidarity Divided: The Crisis in Organized Labor and a New Path toward Social Justice* (Berkeley:

University of California Press, 2008).

3   Raquel Rolnik, "Report of the Special Rapporteur on Adequate Housing as a Component of the right to an adequate standard of living, and on the Right to Non-discrimination in this Context," Human Rights Council of the United Nations General Assembly, http://www.ohchr.org/Documents/Issues/Housing/A-HRC-19-53_en.pdf

4   I first learned of the concept of "insurgent citizenship" when I received a wonderful submission for an anthology on housing, which my co-editor and I were unable to complete. That article found another home: Faranak Miraftaub and Shana Wills, "Insurgency and Spaces of Active Citizenship: The Story of Western Cape Anti-Eviction Campaign in South Africa," *Journal of Planning Education and Research* 25 no. 2 (2005): 200–217.

5   Rob Robinson in conversation with the author.

6   Peter Marcuse and W. Dennis Keating, "The Permanent Housing Crisis: The Failures of Conservatism and the Limitations of Liberalism," in *A Right to Housing: Foundation for a New Social Agenda*, ed. Rachel Bratt et al. (Philadelphia: Temple University Press, 2007).

7   Jason Hackworth, *The Neoliberal City: Governance: Ideology and Development in American Urbanism* (New York: Cornell University Press: 2011), 40.

8   Much of this description takes off from Mike Miller's description of community control and nationalism in the context of the Mission Coalition Organization (Mike Miller, *A Community Organizer's Tale*, 170).

9   Western Regional Advocacy Project, *Without Housing: Decades of Federal Housing Cutbacks, Massive Homelessness and Policy Failures* (San Francisco: WRAP, 2010).

10  Shalia Dewan, "Eminent Domain: A Long Shot against Blight," *New York Times*, January 11, 2014.

11  Darwin Bond Graham, "Grand Theft Banking," *East Bay Express*, February 27, 2013.

12  Andre Gorz, *A Strategy for Labor: A Radical Proposal* (Boston: Beacon Press, 1967)

13  I owe thanks to radical urbanist Tom Wetzel for the many hours of debate and discussion that led me to this conclusion.

14  Anton Weber, quoted in Charles O. Hardy, *The Housing Program of the City of Vienna* (Washington D.C.: Brookings Institution, 1934).

15  Chuck Morse, "Mayor Quan's 102K Housing Plan: Don't Do the Math," http://www.project-oakland.org/mayor-jean-quans-10k2-housing-plan-dont-do-the-math.

16  Most affordable housing in the United States is financed by two engines: fees from for-profit development and tax credits. At this point in
history, both are necessary in order to create needed housing for those
not served by the market. However, both have a conservatizing impact
on the affordable housing sector. The fees (often through inclusionary
housing programs) mean that market-rate housing is built first and
in abundance, followed by a fractional amount of affordable homes.
Tax credits are even more conservative as corporations reduce their tax
burden through investing in affordable housing.

music and musicians, 6, 42, 115
"musical rooms," 39, 40, 132n2
mutual aid networks, 39, 41, 82

**N**

National Advisory Committee on
Civil Disorders. *See* Kerner
Commission
National Guard Armory, 61
National Housing Law Project
(NHLP), 8–9
National Welfare Rights
Organization (NWRO), 45
Native Americans. *See* American
Indians
navy bases, 115
neighbors, 30, 41, 44, 82, 115
–16; of squatters, 20, 21;
in unemployed workers'
movement, 4; wrong
assumptions about, 28
"neoliberalism" (word), 10
New Communist Movement
(NCM), 15
New Communities, 88–89
new housing, 31, 83, 110, 112
*New Mission News*, 132n1
New Orleans, 25, 36, 100
New York City, 44, 86–87, 88,
100, 113
New York City Community
Land Initiative, 86
*New York for Sale: Community
Planning Confronts Global
Real Estate* (Angotti), 113
nonprofit housing, 64, 74, 80, 98,
99–100, 103, 118
North Beach, 23, 24, 26, 27, 36,
66, 96–97, 130n16
North Beach Tenant Association,
36
N.W.A., 33

**O**

Oakland, 106, 112, 134n22
occupation of offices, etc. (tactic),
41, 56, 61, 62, 77, 79. *See also*
squats and occupations
Occupy movement, 35, 104–5
Ohlone people, 63
"One Strike and You're Out" law,
26–27, 129–30n15

**P**

panhandling, 130n18
parks, 73
participatory budgeting, 114–17
patronage, 116–17, 135n28
People Organized to Demand
Environmental and Economic
Rights (PODER), 58, 60, 61,
72–73
Peskin, Aaron, 83
PHTPA. *See* Public Housing
Tenant Protection Act
(PHTPA)
pickets, 19, 72
Picture the Homeless (PTH),
86–87
Pittsburg, 36
Piven, Frances Fox, 45
Poblet, Maria, 62
PODER. *See* People Organized
to Demand Environmental
and Economic Rights
(PODER)
police: New Orleans, 36; San
Francisco, 57, 64; Vallejo, 33
poster campaigns, 57, 58, 66, 68
poverty, 31, 32, 45, 47–48, 87
prison and prisons, 130n20
private property, 63, 90, 102,
110; seizure of, 5, 23. *See also*
property destruction (direct
action)
privatization, 33, 64, 110, 111

# Support **AK Press!**

AK Press is one of the world's largest and most productive anarchist publishing houses. We're entirely worker-run & democratically managed. We operate without a corporate structure—no boss, no managers, no bullshit. We publish close to twenty books every year, and distribute thousands of other titles published by other like-minded independent presses from around the globe.

The Friends of AK program is a way that you can directly contribute to the continued existence of AK Press, and ensure that we're able to keep publishing great books just like this one! Friends pay $25 a month directly into our publishing account ($30 for Canada, $35 for international), and receive a copy of every book AK Press publishes for the duration of their membership! Friends also receive a discount on anything they order from our website or buy at a table: 50% on AK titles, and 20% on everything else. We've also added a new Friends of AK ebook program: $15 a month gets you an electronic copy of every book we publish for the duration of your membership. Combine it with a print subscription, too!

There's great stuff in the works—so sign up now to become a Friend of AK Press, and let the presses roll!

Won't you be our friend? Email friendsofak@akpress.org for more info, or visit the Friends of AK Press website: www.akpress.org/programs/friendsofak